DATE DUE

MAY - 6 1997			

HIGHSMITH   45231

▼▼▼▼▼▼▼

TARGETING
FAMILIES

▲▲▲▲▲▲▲

Marketing To and Through
the New Family

TARGETING FAMILIES

Marketing To and Through the New Family

ROBERT BOUTILIER

AMERICAN
DEMOGRAPHICSBOOKS.

31.45

AMERICAN
DEMOGRAPHICS BOOKS.
A Division of American Demographics, Inc.
127 West State Street, Ithaca, NY 14850
Telephone: 607-273-6343

28601583

65824

HF
5415.1
B68
1993

Executive Editor: Diane Crispell
Associate Editor: Shannon Dortch
Associate Publisher: James Madden
Assistant Editor: Sarah Sirlin
Book Design and Composition: Rebecca Wilson, Anne Kilgore

This publication is designed to provide accurate and authoritative information
in regard to the subject matter covered. It is sold with the understanding that the
publisher is not engaged in rendering legal, accounting, or other professional
services. If legal advice or other expert assistance is required, the services of a
competent professional should be sought.

Hardcover: ISBN 0-936889-22-5
Paperback: ISBN 0-936889-23-3
Library of Congress Catalog Number 93-71268

Cataloging In Publication Data
Boutilier, Robert, 1950–
Targeting families; marketing to and through the new family

To Kai, Del, and Robbie

ACKNOWLEDGMENTS

This book would not have been possible without the support of my family. My wife, Ann, deserves special thanks for her critique of the manuscript. I also thank Diane Crispell of American Demographics Books for her valuable editorial work. I am grateful also to my many friends and colleagues, too numerous to mention individually, who encouraged me to write this book and shared their ideas freely.

Contents

Preface

The aim of this book is to help marketers sell more products and services. Toward that end, it draws together insights from many diverse fields and applies them to the challenges of marketing to and through families.

The first part of the book explains why an understanding of the changing family is increasingly important to marketers. This discussion relies heavily on ideas from economics, developmental psychology, and sociology, especially the field of demography. The second part of the book offers guidance to marketers wishing to take a family marketing approach. It draws on concepts from marketing, consumer psychology, social psychology, advertising, and marketing research.

Lurking in the background at various points in the book is the political controversy over family policy. It is impossible to discuss anything related to family without raising objections from people who are deeply committed to fixed political stances on "the family." I make no pretense of being objective on the subject because I firmly believe that objectivity is impossible to achieve.

The best any of us can probably hope for is a continually expanding awareness of our own presuppositions. We can never stand completely outside of our own perspective. We can, however, try to understand how it has both broadened and limited our thinking. Having said that, I now owe a description of my viewpoint as far as I have been able to discover it.

I suspect that most people are like me, in that the strongest determinants of their views on family are their own personal experience. My family of origin, the one I grew up with in the 1950s and 1960s, is remarkably similar to my family of procreation, the one I formed with my wife. Like my father, I have taken brief turns at being both a full-time breadwinner and homemaker. Still, most of my experience has been with a dual-income family structure.

I have no direct experience with divorce to illuminate my understanding of it. Likewise, I have only limited experience with the distribution of tasks on the basis of gender. This particular combination of modern and traditional experience means that my great personal understanding lies in what is called the "neotraditional" family. Many share my experience, of course, which is why I emphasize the neotraditional family in this book—because it is the most recent development in the history of the North American middle-class family.

It is common to assume that whatever is newest is also better. The idea of improvement or progress is often associated with descriptions of trends or stages of development. Applying these ideas to the evolution of the North American family, one might assume that the modern family was an improvement on the traditional family because it freed individuals from the shackles of tradition. One might further assert that the postmodern family was morally superior to the modern family because it freed women from patriarchal oppression and domestic servitude. Pushing boldly forward, one might argue that the neotraditional family is best of all, because it does everything that previous family forms did, as well as providing a stable protective nexus for rearing children.

I do not read any moral progress into changing family forms, however. Instead, I assume that families change in response to outside forces. I suspect that the strongest external forces are economic. From this perspective, families always have, and always will, adapt to meet the human needs of their members as best they can.

For example, the economic necessities of an agricultural economy made the traditional family a suitable adaptation. In such economies, families are more important as units of production than units of consumption. Spouses value each other's productive abilities in their respective gender-determined spheres.

When the North American economy became industrial, workers had to become more mobile, breaking their traditional connection with the land and moving to cities. Since most industrial jobs paid enough for one wage to support the family, the importance of in-home production for survival decreased. At the same time, the consumptive importance of homemaking increased just when consumer products were becoming a more significant portion of the economy. Thus, the modern "nuclear" family was the best way to manage.

When the economy shifted from production-driven to mostly consumption-driven, opportunities for consumption grew, but so did pressures. Since the homemaking sphere was the arena of consumption, one of the best ways to increase it was to create more households. The divorce boom helped satisfy this economic demand. Although the decline in household size is much more complicated than this, of course, the Nobel-Prize-winning work of Gary Becker nonetheless implicates affluence as at least one contributing cause of divorce.

Another economic change that probably contributed to the rise of postmodern diversity in family forms was the rise of the knowledge-based economy. As information overtook manufacturing in job creation, women found increasing opportunities for agreeable employment. Since more of them had become self-supporting singles and single parents, many were eager to take advantage of these opportunities.

During the 1980s, the debt-inflated bubble of consumption burst. Married women with children at home joined divorced and single women in the full-time work force. Dual incomes were not enough, however, to raise real household incomes. Economic stagnation and recession gave rise to the neotraditional family.

The neotraditional family is depicted as wanting to get "back to basics," as if this was a choice based on a shift in values. I see this as an attempt to make a virtue out of necessity. People in neotraditional families are getting back to basics because they cannot afford the independence from one another that those in postmodern families had. Staying together and working through marital difficulties seems on the surface a reaffirmation of lifelong commitment. In fact, it may also be more financially feasible than getting divorced.

The fact that the economy has undergone several massive structural changes in the 20th century probably accounts for the high level of family diversity we see today. The family forms that were suited to older economic arrangements persist, while new adaptive forms have arisen alongside them. While the political and moral debates about family structure rage around us, professional marketers can still step back and scan the social landscape for profitable opportunities. The time is right for developing our thinking about the implications of family structure for marketing. With that in mind, I have tried to raise questions as much as I have offered guidance and helpful advice.

—Robert Boutilier
Burnaby, British Columbia
April 1993

PART I

The Importance of "Family"

CHAPTER ONE

Today's Families and How They Got the Way They Are

Family marketing does not replace existing marketing knowledge and practice. The tried-and-true methods still work. But by providing a new way of looking at problems, it offers a new perspective on marketing challenges and leads to new ways of applying marketing techniques, for better results.

In family marketing, the purchase decision maker may not be an individual, but a social group. In fact, "influencers" may be as important to purchases as decision makers. Family marketing is directed not only "to" families, but "through" them.

By marketing "to" families, I refer to buying decisions made by all family members for their shared consumption, such as vacations, pizzas, or brands of toothpaste. All members of the family need not have equal input or interest in the decision. But when family members communicate about the decision, the family makes the decision and collectively functions as the buying unit.

Marketing "through" the family describes messages directed to relatives and family members living in other households. These include trans-generational influences (e.g., empty-nest parents influencing their adult children's home furnishing choices), extended-family influences (e.g., "Let's ask Uncle George where to get the insurance we need"), and step-family influences (e.g., grandparents buying roller blades for their remarried son's new step-children). When family members from other households affect the decision of the purchaser, market influences are channeled *through* them.

Many people have highly emotional reactions to the word "family." Some insist that "family" can only mean a nuclear family, consisting of a husband, a wife, and their children. Childless couples and single parents do not qualify. At the other extreme, some hear the word "family" as a code word for intolerant values and patriarchal attitudes. They argue for defining "family" so that it includes diverse units, such as unwed single parents and their children and childless cohabiting couples, whether they be heterosexual or homosexual. Perhaps the only unit that would not meet the politically correct definition of family is singles living alone.

In this book, "family" is used to mean something less inclusive than "household" but more inclusive than a traditional nuclear family. It also means more than a "couple." Here, "family" means a social unit that meets at least one of the following criteria: (a) emotionally connected cohabiting people with at least one parent-child type relationship (e.g., caretaking, nurturing) between two of them, and/or (b) people related by blood or marriage.

During the past two decades, American families have become much more diverse in their composition, structure, and functioning. But they are no less important to their members. The intent in this book is to acknowledge the variety of reactions people have to the family and to help marketers take account of those diverse reactions when practicing family marketing.

Buying Decisions as Effects of Social Interaction

Family marketing asserts the importance of both the individual and the family in purchase decisionmaking. The person who signs the credit-card receipt does not necessarily make the purchase decision in isolation. Strictly individualistic approaches to marketing ignore the enormous number of purchase decisions people make through the interpersonal process of consensus building.

Industrial marketers have been less likely to ignore group influences on purchases. They know that industrial buyers tend to use agreed-upon decision criteria. Even when a company has no explicit criteria-defining process, the buyers who survive and thrive are those who factor the preferences of internal stakeholders, such as workers and the comptroller, into the decision. Sophisticated industrial marketers try to understand the internal company forces that act upon the buyer and craft their products and messages accordingly. For consumer products and services, the analog of the company is the family.

Diversity in Family Structures

From time to time, news stories appear announcing the death of the "family." A closer look usually reveals that the author has used a very narrow definition of family. The nuclear family, consisting of a married couple with children at home, is indeed in decline. By 1990, married couples with children who comprised 41 percent of all households in 1970 had diminished to only 27 percent. When "family" is more broadly defined, the real story that emerges is about changes in the proportions of family types. Many different schemes classify today's diverse families. Sociologists and social anthropologists interested in kinship networks are more likely to use classification systems based on blood relationships. Marketers, however, are more interested in financial and lifestyle factors like income and household composition. Gordon Green and Edward Welniak of the U.S. Bureau of the Census use the nine-category system illustrated on the next page.

The decline in the proportion of

▶ **Family Diversity**

Families have become much more diverse in the past few decades, but they are just as important as ever to the people who live in them.

Fewer Traditional Family Households

(change in percent of all households, 1970 to 1990)

	households	household incomes
Dual-earner married couples with children (two-earner parents)	-1 %	0 %
Other married couples with children (single-earner or no-earner parents)	-13	-16
Childless married couples with householders under age 45 (young couples)	+1	+2
Childless married couples with householders aged 45 to 64 (empty nesters)	-2	0
Childless married couples with householders aged 65 and older (mature couples)	0	+2
Single parents	+3	+2
Childless singles under age 45 (young singles)	+6	+4
Childless singles aged 45 and older (older singles)	+2	+3
Other multiple-member (shared households)	+4	+4

Source: Census Bureau

single-earner families with children is mostly attributable to the massive entry of women into the work force. In 1960, 61 percent of married couples consisted of a male breadwinner and a female home-maker. In 1990, only 22 percent of married couples had this arrangement. During the same period, the proportion of single-parent families increased. In 1960, only 10 percent of American children lived with a single parent. By 1990, it was 22 percent. The proportion of single-parent households rose from 6 percent of all households in 1970 to 9 percent in 1990.

The shift away from marriage has been even more dramatic in Canada, where single parents and unmarried couples get tax and social assistance advantages over married couples with children. Between 1984 and 1990, the share of Canadians aged 18 to 64 who had ever lived in a common-law marriage doubled, from 6 percent to 12 percent.

In a related development, the number of U.S. men living outside of families also increased dramatically. "Bachelors" include never-married, divorced, and widowed men. In 1987, they accounted for 34 percent of American men older than age 18. During the 1980s, the number of bachelors in the United States increased by approximately 21 percent. Bachelors have become a more diverse group in the past two decades, as more middle-aged bachelors have been added to the younger "wild and crazy guys." This "bachelor boom" has contributed to another interesting development, the surge in nonfamily shared households. From 1970 to 1990, nonfamily shared households increased from 6 percent to 10 percent of all households.

This diversification into increasingly smaller and nonfamily households might suggest that the family is becoming less, rather than more important to people. After reviewing many studies, however, Martha Farnsworth Riche of the Population Reference Bureau in Washington, D.C., came to a different conclusion. In a March 1991 article in *American Demographics* magazine, she says:

> As marriage becomes less central to family life, children and other relatives become increasingly important. This remains true even after the children are grown. Family members, present or absent, provide the major focus of social life and social support. These functions are all the more important as individuals live increasingly separate and increasingly long lives.

The "family household" is a more diverse and short-lived institution than it used to be, but family influences are no less important in buying decisions. Today's

▶ **Family Influence**

Families still influence buying decisions as much as they always have, but in a different way.

variations in family structure, however, do make a big difference in *how* families influence buying decisions. In families that live together under one roof, members are likely to express their influences directly. In families scattered across two or more households, the influences more often operate at the level of quasi-conscious yearnings, identifications, hostilities, and anxieties.

In the past, marketers have sporadically taken account of family influences on buying decisions. The image of the traditional nuclear family is one of a breadwinning father, a homemaking mother, and at least two children. They all live in a suburban house. Neither parent has been married previously. In the 1950s and 1960s, marketers took advantage of this predictable pattern to simplify their strategies. They never worried about selling household cleaners to men. They created TV ads in which hubby and the kids praised mom for using the right product. They did door-to-door surveys during the daytime to interview "the woman of the house." In a sense, their family marketing strategy relied upon their intimate familiarity with a single family structure to increase sales.

In the 1970s, those patterns changed. The divorce boom was in full swing. New households formed rapidly, and the average household size continued to decline. Door-to-door daytime surveys began to be misleading. Because it looked like the disappearance of traditional roles meant the disappearance of family bonds, more and more marketers targeted individuals, rather than families.

But even though traditional roles and structures are now the exception, the emotional bonds and interpersonal influences that operate within families are as strong as ever. A single mother deciding on a sofa is likely to take into account what her own mother will think of the choice before buying. In personal interviews about such purchase decisions, I found women wondering, "If the style is too contemporary, will my mom think I haven't created a 'real' home for the children?"

Sometimes family influence works to the detriment of a product. A young male student renting with a roommate might want to seem independent of parental influences. Try selling him his father's favorite brand of beer, and he won't touch it. He wants to distance himself from his parents and their way of life. The fact that parental

Single Parents

As the divorce rates rose and more women had children out of wedlock, the share of single-parent families more than tripled between 1960 and 1990.

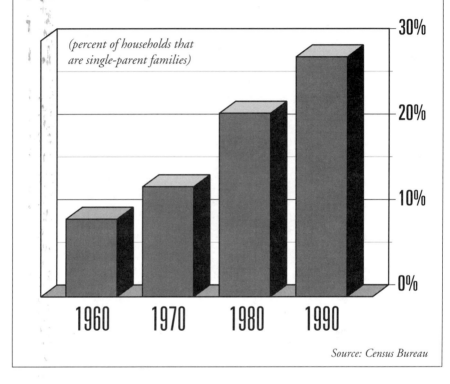

(percent of households that are single-parent families)

30%

20%

10%

0%

1960   1970   1980   1990

Source: Census Bureau

influence is operating in reverse does not make it less powerful. A marketer targeting such a "rebellious" segment should play up themes related to generational differences and independence. This positioning will work *because of* family influences, not in spite of them.

Empty-nester couples are among the smallest of today's households, consisting as they do of a married couple whose children have grown and left. The small size of these households, however, does not reflect their influence within families. Empty nesters are often more likely to initiate contact with family members in other households and may take on more responsibility for their own elderly parents. Many are also grandparents. When it comes to toys and cloth-

Traditional Period: Pre-1925

Smaller				Larger
Fewer Generations				More Generations
Natural Father Present				Natural Father Absent
Atomized	Distanced Household	Independent Nuclear	Nondomiciled Extended	Domiciled Extended

(Shaded is "mainstream.")

ing for grandchildren, they may go shopping with their own adult children or do the shopping themselves.

Families have changed a great deal over the past three decades. But if we look at a longer period, we see that today's family diversity is only a momentary transition in a much larger pendulum swing of change in family structure.

A Continuum of Family Structures

The family and household structures we see today can be crudely arrayed along a continuum from small, loose-knit family households to large, close-knit extended-family households.

"Atomized" households include bachelor roommates, singles, and childless couples. "Distanced" households include single mothers and their children, blended families, and cohabitants with children. Atomized and distanced households account for most of growing family diversity. On average, they are small households with as little as a single generation living together. They are less likely to contain a natural father and his own children.

The fabled but fading nuclear family falls in the middle of today's family spectrum. It includes two generations, parents and children. The children's natural father is part of the household.

Larger family households are at the far end of the spectrum. The "nondomiciled extended" household looks much like the independent nuclear family, but actively participates in many activities

Modern Period: 1925–1975

| Smaller | | | | Larger |
| Fewer Generations | | | | More Generations |
Natural Father Present				Natural Father Absent
Atomized	Distanced Household	Independent Nuclear	Nondomiciled Extended	Domiciled Extended

(Shaded is "mainstream.")

with extended-family members. Grandparents, aunts, and uncles may live within walking distance. Two households with grown siblings might share a small business or summer cottage. Frequent family gatherings include family members from several households.

The "domiciled extended" family looks like the Waltons. They are close-knit, as is the case with recently arrived immigrants in many ethnic groups. Family loyalty often takes precedence over individual preferences. The longer such an ethnic family has been in North America, the closer the youngest generation moves toward the center of the continuum. This continuum is an abstraction. Real-life families do not fall into neat abstract categories. A pair of sisters, both single mothers living with their parents, look like a domiciled extended family, even though the natural fathers of the third generation are absent.

The position of the "mainstream" family structure along this continuum changes through time. Through most of the 20th century, it has edged to the left, toward "atomization" and "distancing." But today's families are moving to the right, toward extended kinship relations. As a result, the mainstream consumer in the 1990s is more responsive to marketing that addresses family relations.

Before the 1920s, the American family was in a stage of evolution that Professor William J. Doherty of the University of Minnesota, in a 1992 *Psychology Today* article calls the "institutional family." It was characterized by tradition-oriented commitments to work, kin, and community. The father was the family authority, and people viewed marriage more as a functional, social, and economic arrangement than as an outcome of romantic love. The chief value in the institutional family was responsibility.

Doherty describes the family form that emerged in the "modern" period (1925 to 1975) as the "psychological family." The "hot button" for the psychological family was personal satisfaction. Increasing rural–urban migration early in the period broke kinship and community ties, and the family became a self-contained unit, the nuclear family. The economic benefits of marriage were supplanted by psychological benefits like love, attraction, and companionship.

Other commentators use different labels for the family of this period. Psychology professor David Elkind of Tufts University calls it the "modern family." His nomenclature derives from the more general discourse in social philosophy regarding the shift from the "modern" to the "postmodern" era. Between 1965 and 1975, the modern era was superseded by the postmodern era. In a nutshell, that means we threw out the "modern" notion that differences of opinion in social, cultural, and moral discourse result from different groups viewing the same basic truths from different vantage points, and instead, we adopted the "postmodern" assumption that no basic truths exist and that all social behaviors, standards, attitudes, and beliefs are equally valid.

Elkind applies the modern/postmodern dichotomy to family structures. He describes the modern family in terms of three main sentiments. In his view, the first is romantic love, the feeling that legitimizes ignoring community and parental influences in the mate-selection process. Romantic love supposedly allows an individual to see the "true" person beyond the stereotypes about social class, race, etc. The second sentiment is maternal love. This revolves around the idea that women have a need or "instinct" to care for children. The third sentiment is domesticity. According to this notion, "relationships within the family are always more powerful than those outside it." In other words, blood is thicker than water. This modernist assumption imbues family relationships with a transcultural, transhistorical importance.

The postmodern family is also called "pluralistic" (Doherty) or "permeable" (Elkind). According to Doherty, its chief value is

Postmodern Period: 1975–1990

Smaller Fewer Generations Natural Father Present				Larger More Generations Natural Father Absent
Atomized	Distanced Household	Independent Nuclear	Nondomiciled Extended	Domiciled Extended

(Shaded is "mainstream." Note the optimal diversity in what constitutes "mainstream.")

flexibility. It celebrates tolerance and diversity. From childhood to old age, children born in this era move in and out of family forms throughout their lives. They may be born into a two-parent nuclear family that becomes a single-parent family and later becomes a blended family. They may grow up to cohabit, marry, divorce, cohabit again, and marry again.

Elkind points out that the postmodern family is not as closed to outside influences as the modern family was. Why should it be if, as a postmodernist would assume, all types of close relationships can be equally important? Whereas the institutional family was open to influences from the church and kinship network, the postmodern family delegates its responsibilities to day-care centers, schools, social workers, police, charitable organizations, government agencies, and television. Elkind notes that the postmodern family is so permeable to outside influences that it cannot protect children from the harsh realities of life. Instead, the postmodern family has led the trend toward crediting children with more competence and judgment. Movies like *Home Alone* reflect this trend. Children not only have equal rights with adults, they also have equal abilities. Elkind feels that by pressuring children to take care of themselves, the postmodern family errs on the side of neglecting their emotional needs.

Doherty sees a new family form emerging in the 1990s, but does not name it. For the purposes of this discussion, I have dubbed it the "neotraditional family." Characteristic of this new form are commitment, care, community, equality, and diversity. The neotra-

Neotraditional Period: Beyond 1990

Smaller Fewer Generations Natural Father Present			More Generations Natural Father Absent Larger	
Atomized	Distanced Household	Independent Nuclear	Nondomiciled Extended	Domiciled Extended

(Shaded is "mainstream.")

ditional family combines elements of the modern family and the postmodern family. It maintains the postmodern tolerance for diversity. At the same time, it reflects the modern assumption that family relations are more important than nonfamily relations.

Back to Basics

The historical duration of the postmodern family is a matter of conjecture. For most who grew up in postmodern families, any other type of family life may seem unfamiliar or strange. They may not want to follow the neotraditional trend. Nonetheless, others are eager to get "back to basics" in family life.

Sociologist Frances Goldscheider documents many ways in which families have become more loose-knit over the past 20 years. Americans spend less of their lives in family households than ever before. The postmodern family includes not only nonnuclear families, but also the "no family" option that Goldscheider and co-author Linda Waite describe in their 1991 book *New Families, No Families?*

Perhaps because of this family deprivation, Americans are increasingly drawn to close-knit families. Three societal changes underlie this trend. First, baby boomers are entering the stage of life where family concerns are inescapable. Second, the financial cost of breaking away from the family has increased relative to income. This increasingly common circumstance forces more people to live in larger households and families. Third, most immigrants now come from cultures that are more family-oriented than late 20th-century American culture. Moreover, the second and third generations in today's immigrant families face less pressure than earlier in this century to adopt individualistic attitudes and lifestyles. Let's look at each of these changes in more detail.

The baby-boom cohort (born 1946 to 1964), is aging. Researchers and trend trackers have noticed that boomers are changing as they enter middle age. They are not "doing" middle age exactly the same way their parents did but are returning to selected aspects of traditional values. Like middle-aged persons in all times and cultures, American boomers today must deal with the dual responsibilities of growing children and aging parents. These responsibilities make people more family oriented. As the largest and best-educated cohort in society, their changing values tend to ripple outward, affecting other generations.

The last time the U.S. had a trade surplus was in April 1976. This was a turning point in American history, because it suggests that the U.S. peaked as a world economic power almost 20 years ago. Some observers, like Yale historian Paul Kennedy, see the U.S. in a long slow decline. Marketers must determine how Americans will adapt to no longer being the richest nation on earth. One adaptation is a sure bet. Americans will do what people in less affluent countries have always done—live in larger households.

> ## ▶ Boomers and Family
>
> As baby boomers reach middle age, their dual responsibilities toward young children and elderly parents are making them more family oriented.

This trend has already begun. For most of the 20th century, the size of American households has been shrinking. In 1983, however, the tide turned. Average household size increased that year, then continued to decline. Analysts thought it was a temporary blip attributable to the recession, but in 1990, household size grew again. With almost two decades of trade deficits, the U.S. can expect at least another decade of frequent recessions and slower recoveries. With each recession, the average size of American households will likely increase. This will happen through divorces being put off and through adult children living longer with their parents.

In the past, immigrants to the U.S. were from family-oriented cultures. Lower standards of living in the "old countries" necessitated a strong commitment to family. More important, the cultures from which today's immigrants come are even more family oriented than in the past. Recent immigrants to North America are likely to be Asian or Hispanic. These cultures imbue their members with a loyalty to the family, and individual wishes take second place to family needs. Both of these broad ethnic groups are gaining in economic strength. Their importance in the marketplace is growing, while the proportion of non-Hispanic white consumers is decreasing. Appealing to these consumers requires an understanding of their deep commitment to the family.

Although Americans are becoming more family-oriented, dramatic change will not happen overnight. Families satisfy the most basic of human needs, and within their bounds, family members learn the fundamental concepts of love and belonging. These notions begin to take root even before children learn to talk. Such deeply rooted ideas do not change quickly or even at all.

The return to more close-knit family forms will not be rapid. It will gather momentum slowly because it affects so many diverse aspects of our culture and daily lives. The gradual nature of change in family structure suggests that family marketing can be key to a company's long-term marketing strategy. The slow changes are the ones that last and are the farthest-reaching.

REFERENCES

Cutler, Blayne. "Bachelor Boom." *American Demographics*, February 1989, p. 24.

Davis, John. "Wall $treet Week with Louis Rukeyser." December 27, 1991. Owings Mills, MD: Maryland Public Television.

Doherty, William J. "Private Lives, Public Values: The New Pluralism—A Report from the Heartland." *Psy-*

chology Today, Vol. 25, No. 3, May/June 1992, pp. 33-37, 82.

Exter, Thomas. "Average Household Size Up for the First Time in Seven Years." *American Demographics*, January 1991, p. 10.

Gergen, Kenneth J. *The Saturated Self: Dilemmas of Identity in Contemporary Life.* New York: Basic Books, 1982.

Goldscheider, Frances K. and Linda J. Waite. *New Families, No Families? The Transformation of the American Home.* Berkeley, CA: University of California Press, 1991.

Green, Gordon, and Edward Welniak. "The Nine Household Markets." *American Demographics*, October 1991, p. 38.

Harvey, David. *The Condition of Postmodernity.* Cambridge, MA: Basil Blackwell, Inc., 1990.

Hughes, John. *Home Alone.* Beverly Hills, CA: Twentieth Century Fox, 1990.

Jameson, Fredric. *Postmodernism: Or the Cultural Logic of Late Capitalism.* Durham, NC: Duke University Press, 1991.

Kennedy, Paul. *The Rise and Fall of Great Powers.* New York: Random House, 1988.

Lyotard, Jean-Francois. *The Postmodern Condition: A Report on Knowledge.* Minneapolis, MN: University of Minnesota Press, 1979.

McGowan, John. *Postmodernism and Its Critics.* Ithaca, NY: Cornell University Press, 1991.

Riche, Martha Farnsworth. "The Future of the Family." *American Demographics*, March 1991, pp. 44, 46.

Sandler, Marilyn. "The Consumer of the '90s." *Marketline*, September 1990, pg. 4.

REFERENCES

Sandler, Marilyn. "The Consumer of the '90s." *Marketline*, November 1990, pg. 4.

Schaie, K. Warner and Sherry L. Willis. *Adult Development and Aging*, 2/e. Glenview, IL: Scott, Foresman & Co., 1986.

Stout, Cam. "Common Law: A Growing Alternative." *Canadian Social Trends*, Winter 1991, pp. 18-20.

Strauss, William and Neil Howe. *Generations: The History of America's Future, 1584 to 2069*. New York: William Morrow and Company, 1991.

U.S. Bureau of the Census. *U.S. Census of Population, 1970* (PC-2-4A), and *Current Population Reports*, Series P-20, No. 458 and earlier reports.

Waldrop, Judith, and Thomas Exter. "What the 1990 Census Will Show." *American Demographics*, January 1990, p. 27.

CHAPTER TWO

Boomers and Post-Boomers

In the 1990s, baby boomers will be squeezed between getting their parents into nursing homes and getting their kids into college. Some will begin baby-sitting their own grandchildren. Baby boomers have always had a large impact on popular culture and the social agenda. Because baby boomers are human, their progression into middle age is bound to raise the level of social concern for the family.

At the same time, the post-boomer generation will enter young adulthood, the most independence-oriented phase of life. Because such a large proportion of them grew up in unstable family situations, they will fear abandonment more and furtively crave secure relationships more than the baby boomers did. They will be less strident about the value of "do-your-own-thing" self-sufficiency than the baby boomers were during young adulthood.

The boomers were the product of the baby-making frenzy that followed the death and destruction of World War II. The boundaries of that generation can be set by looking at fertility rates.

Fertility-rate data set the boundary differently in different countries. In the United States, Australia, New Zealand, and Canada, fertility rose about one-half child per woman from 1945 to 1947. Rates then leveled off or dropped until about 1951. In Canada and the United States, fertility "spiked" sharply in 1947. From 1951 to about 1961, these four countries had steadily rising fertility rates. Between 1962 and 1966, fertility suddenly plummeted to around the 1945 level. The U.S. boom includes everyone born between 1946 and 1964. In the year 2000, these people will be aged 36 to 54.

By contrast, in western European countries like France, Germany, Belgium, Austria, and the United Kingdom, there was no post-war spike, fertility rates were lower overall, and the boom did not end until around 1971. In Ireland in the late 1950s, fertility was comparable to, or higher than in the United States, Australia, New Zealand, and Canada. The Irish, however, maintained these high levels until about 1975.

In their 1991 book *Generations: The History of America's Future*, William Strauss and Neil Howe define "Generation 13" as those born between 1961 and 1981. Thirteeners are also known as post-boomers, "Generation X," and the baby bust. The variety of labels for this generation manifests their predicament. Coming as they did in the shadow of the baby boom, one of their prime characteristics is the lack of a strong generational identity. One thing these people have in common is that they were born during the period from about 1966 to 1982, when fertility rates were either falling steadily or flat, at levels far below those of the late-1940s to mid-1960s. As a result, the post-boomers are a small group.

> ► **Boomer Issues**
>
> Social issues of the past few decades have in large part paralleled the concerns of the baby-boom generation. Today's big topic: parenting.

Baby boomers have always been a disproportionately large group in the U.S., where they make up one-third of the population. As a result, social concerns in the past 25 years have paralleled their concerns. When they were children in the 1950s and 1960s, popular culture was family-oriented, Ozzie and Harriet ruled the TV ratings, and wave after wave of toy and dance fads rolled across the land. Boomers entered the serious mate-selection stage in the late

1960s and 1970s. Right on cue, American popular culture was about "sex and drugs and rock and roll." In the 1980s, boomers got haircuts and jobs. Their watchwords became success and ambition. Business publications blossomed, and women wore "power suits" with shoulder pads. In the mid-1990s, even the youngest of the boomers is turning "thirtysomething." They are now a parent boom. A growing number are grandparents. Understanding the workings of the middle-aged mind will help us anticipate the future influence of boomers in the consumer marketplace.

The Middle-Aged Mind

Psychoanalyst Erik Erikson has developed a lifespan theory of human development that portrays middle age as a distinct stage of life. Contemporary social scientists studying lifespan human development have confirmed many of Erikson's hypotheses and have added some new insights. This body of knowledge provides a clear, consistent picture of where boomers are going. Erikson took his psychoanalytic training with Anna Freud, Sigmund's daughter. After coming to the U.S., he taught at Harvard Medical School, Yale, and Berkeley. He broke with traditional Freudianism by placing more importance on the ego and on a person's abilities to solve problems rationally and to adjust to changing life circumstances. Erikson's theory was the first in psychology to consider human development across the entire lifespan. He is perhaps most famous for developing the concept of the "identity crisis."

Up to puberty, the stages of ego development in Erikson's theory follow roughly the same chronological sequence as Freud's. The "identity crisis" occurs anywhere from age 12 to 20. It is immediately followed by the "intimacy crisis," a stage in which a person deals with the challenges of forming a long-term love relationship. By the time people master that monumental task, they are middle-aged. The "generativity crisis" is the ego-development challenge of middle age. In old age, people's attempts to make sense of their lives are part of the "integrity crisis." The strength people develop by resolving the intimacy crisis is the capacity for love. The strength they develop by struggling with the generativity crisis is the capacity for caring and nurturance. Wisdom is the result of the integrity crisis of old age.

Erikson described the caring that develops in middle age as a widening concern for others and an overcoming of ambivalence toward obligations to others. The term "generativity" derives from the growing ability of the middle-aged to set aside immediate self-interest in favor of future generations. During middle age, parents make sacrifices for their children's future. Such people are more likely to engage in volunteer community work and to want to make their part of the world a better place to live. Environmental concerns demonstrate middle-agers' efforts to make sacrifices in the present to hand along a better future.

Erikson was the first to theorize about middle age, a period he saw as lasting from age 25 to 65. Today, most theorists define middle age as the period from age 40 to 65. Many things Erikson said about middle age are more descriptive of the earlier part of the range of middle age as he defined it.

▶ **Defining Middle Age**

Today's concept of middle age derives from psychoanalyst Erik Erikson's lifespan theory of human development, although its age range has moved up.

Warner Schaie, a developmental psychologist, has presented his own theory of thinking styles across the human lifespan. He describes early middle age, from about 25 to 40, as a time when human thinking moves beyond the "acquisitive" style of childhood and the "achieving" style of young adulthood, and becomes more "responsible." This responsibility is to serve one's family and co-workers. In later middle age (ages 40 to 65), thinking styles may change again (but not necessarily). The style can become "executive" as people apply mental skills managing groups or thinking about community affairs that extend beyond the family. In old age, people's thinking becomes "reintegrative," or oriented toward reviewing and making sense of the past.

Recently, social scientists have examined Erikson's and Schaie's theories in more detail. In particular, they have contrasted the idea that middle-aged people focus first on family, and then on community, with the notion that middle-aged people have fewer contacts with their children and parents, and become preoccupied with their own aging, health, and unrealized aspirations. Generally, the view of middle age as a time of self-absorption and transgenerational isolation is a myth. Nonetheless, mere aging does not guarantee that people will develop the middle-aged attributes of caring and social responsibility. In politically repressive societies, people simply have fewer opportunities for socially responsible community involvement. But given a responsive social environment and successful adjustment during earlier life stages, people are likely to develop these attributes in middle age.

Concern for Family and Community

Eighty-four percent of respondents in a 1990 study commissioned by the American Board of Family Practice agreed that "at middle age, a person becomes more compassionate to the needs of others." For many, this happens when they become parents. Gerontologist Barbara Payne says that the baby boomers who gave us record numbers of households with childless couples have had enough of independence and self-indulgence. They are now looking for something more substantial than instant gratification.

Parents include fathers as well as mothers. Isobel Osius is marketing research manager at Condé Nast Publications Inc., which publishes *GQ, Bride's, Self,* and *House and Garden,* among other magazines. Her job is to keep track of the interests, enthusiasms, anxieties, and problems of different market segments. In a 1990 national survey of 1,285 men, Osius found that 84 percent ranked family as most important in their lives. That was a significant and sudden increase over the 73 percent of men who ranked family first in 1988. Such a surge over a short period of time suggests a strong trend.

No longer is the conflict between job and family strictly a woman's problem. James Levine, founding director of The Fatherhood Project in New York City, does workshops with employees who are fathers. These workshops deal with issues related to balancing homelife and a career. In some cases, a two- or three-day pro-

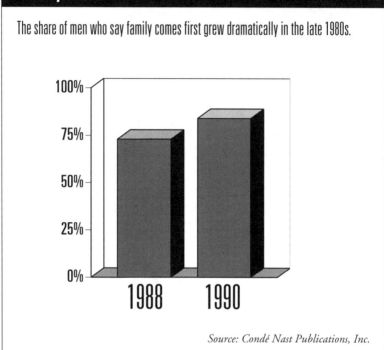

Family Men

The share of men who say family comes first grew dramatically in the late 1980s.

100%

75%

50%

25%

0%

1988   1990

Source: Condé Nast Publications, Inc.

gram stretches into two or three weeks because of overwhelming demand. Levine has found that many men hide the strain of this conflict from their bosses and co-workers.

Caring for children is not the only strain in middle age. Elderly parents become a responsibility, too. In 1985, most caregivers for people aged 75 and older with activity limitations were children or relatives other than a spouse. Middle-aged children are usually the ones who take responsibility for finding and arranging care. From 1980 to 1990, nongovernment spending on nursing-home care increased from $9.5 billion to $25.5 billion, an increase of 268 percent without adjusting for inflation. During the same period, nongovernment spending on home health care increased from $0.4 billion to $1.8 billion, an increase of 450 percent without adjusting for inflation. Clearly, the financial burden of caring for the elderly has grown dramatically.

Some evidence suggests that despite, or perhaps because of, their family commitments, baby boomers want to spend more time maintaining a social life. A 1991 Gallup Poll found that 43 percent of baby-boom women (aged 26 to 45) and 33 percent of baby-boom men plan to decrease their job commitments over the next five years, while 11 percent of men and 23 percent of women plan to quit work completely. One of the things they plan to do with their extra time is seek more and better friendships (59 percent of men and 52 percent of women).

The political aspects of community involvement tend to become stronger in 50-to-65-year-olds. Since most boomers are now in early middle age, their political activities have had to fit into after-work schedules already crammed with little-league baseball practices, children's piano lessons, and endless shopping trips. This may be why recent years have seen a rise in "cause"-related marketing, especially green marketing. Cause marketing and green marketing may have been successful because they gave today's enormous cohort of early middle agers a chance to act on their community concerns. Boomers with children could not avoid shopping malls, but they could politicize them.

Most boomers have yet to undertake more serious community involvement. In the late 1960s and the 1970s, before they had children, many participated in mass protests of various sorts. Those without children are more likely to have continued with political activities begun in the 1970s. Those with children, however, are not likely to be active again until the baby boomlet is in high school, around the turn of the century.

> ►**Cause Marketing**
>
> People become more involved in their communities in middle age. This may be why recent years have seen a rise in "cause-related" marketing, especially green marketing.

In sum, boomers are following the normal human developmental pattern for mid-life. They are finding more value in family, friends, and community.

Thirteeners/Post-Boomers

Isobel Osius sees post-boomers as a group whose needs have been ignored. While these "13ers" were growing up, the American divorce rate more than doubled. When they were children, one-third to two-fifths of post-boomers experienced a parental divorce.

As children of divorce, many 13ers were plunged into poverty, and neglect. The economic impact of divorce on women and the children who live with them is dramatic and sudden. A study by Professor John Robinson of the University of Maryland finds that children of single parents receive four to six hours less parental care per week than do children in two-parent families. Single parents simply do not have the same amount of time or resources to give their children.

During the 1960s, 1970s, and 1980s, psychologists, sociologists, educators, and social workers claimed that divorce's ill effects on children would dissipate in a few years. It now appears that was wishful thinking based on short-term studies. In a long-term study on the effects of divorce, Dr. Judith Wallerstein followed parents and children of 60 divorced families in the San Francisco area from 1971 to 1981. These families, selected for a positive post-divorce prognosis, were all white middle-class families. None of the divorces had been caused by alcoholism or physical abuse. No family members were in therapy at the time of the divorce.

Five years after divorce, Wallerstein found the usual pattern of a satisfactory readjustment after the initial period of trauma—for the adults. But only one-third of the children were unequivocally doing well. More than one-third suffered from a wide variety of behavioral problems, including depression. After ten years, many of the children were young adults. They fit the typical Generation 13 personality profiled by Strauss and Howe in 1991. Wallerstein found two in five young men were drifting, without clear goals. Two-thirds of the young women were afraid of commitment or betrayal. About 60 percent of the young adults felt rejected by at least one parent, usually their father.

During the 1970s, according to Strauss and Howe, the number of latchkey children doubled. These post-boomers came home to empty houses in record numbers because so many of their mothers had joined the work force. Between 1970 and 1987, when 13ers were preschoolers, the share of women who worked during their prime childbearing years (25 to 34) shot up from just over 40 percent to almost 75 percent.

Unfortunately, changes in family status have coincided with record levels of childhood suicide. Strauss and Howe point out that about 5,000 children under the age of 18 committed suicide each year during the 1980s. The rate of suicide among young Canadian men has quadrupled since the 1950s and doubled for young Canadian women.

Violent death outside military service has plagued Generation 13 more than any other living cohort of Americans. Strauss and Howe note that homicide is the primary cause of death among inner-city youth, and that approximately 135,000 urban school children carry guns to school every day.

Not only is the threat to physical safety at an all-time high for Generation 13, but the hope for a better tomorrow is slimmer than it was for previous generations. Throughout the 1950s and 1960s, the age group with the highest poverty rate was aged 65 and older. Since 1974, however, the highest poverty rate has been among children under the age of 18.

> ▶ **Children of Divorce**
>
> As children of divorce, many 13ers were plunged into poverty and neglect.

The neglect, underprotection, and sheer terror thrust upon this generation takes its toll. Thirteeners show types of stress-related pathologies unknown to older generations. One more disturbing characteristic of many children of divorce is the "overburdened child syndrome." Wallerstein found that ten years after divorce, 25 percent of mothers and 20 percent of fathers suffered diminished parenting capacity. They leaned more heavily on their children, and as a result, 15 percent of their children developed burnout reactions because they were overburdened with adult responsibilities.

Other children develop eating disorders, such as anorexia nervosa. Scattered statistics indicate a dramatic increase in this serious problem. Vancouver Children's Hospital in Vancouver, British Columbia, recorded a 300 percent increase in the number of cases from 1980 to 1989. Doctors treating teenagers afflicted with anorexia blame, among other things, increasing pressures on teens to excel. Teenage girls in particular face new pressures because they are expected to prepare for roles as breadwinners in addition to everything else.

The high rate of divorce and latchkey neglect leads many 13ers to be ambivalent about family life. To many, self-sufficiency seems more desirable because one can avoid being neglected, stressed, or overburdened. At the same time, most 13ers recognize that the single-parent family is a perfect recipe for stress. They might, as Isobel Osius predicts, be very receptive to visions of the egalitarian family. Such portrayals will probably be even more powerful if they include emotional appeals to being protected and cherished.

For now, 13ers are still struggling to establish their careers and independence from their parents. Most have not yet started their own families. They are not particularly "pro-family" at this point in their lives, even though they have moved in that direction. Osius finds that, in 1990, only two-thirds of 13er men born between 1966 and 1972 rated family as most important. Although this is a smaller share than the 87 percent for boomer men born before 1956, it is much higher than it was two years earlier (55 percent).

Thirteeners are not as pro-independence as baby boomers were in young adulthood. Based on focus groups with teens, Eric Blais of the Toronto ad agency Harrod & Mirlin Inc. says teens today are less rebellious than more idealistic boomers were at that age.

Thirteeners with higher financial hopes are likely to delay family formation. Young adults who want to meet the educational requirements of today's job market must endure a longer period of dependence on their parents than earlier generations needed, which may be part of the reason why post-boomers are staying longer in their parents' homes. It might also explain why they are marrying later than previous generations did.

Generation 13 may be less predisposed toward divorce than early boomers and pre-boomers. Women's attitudes are probably a

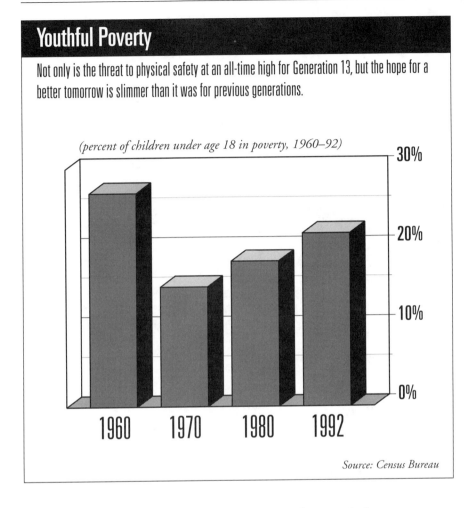

Youthful Poverty

Not only is the threat to physical safety at an all-time high for Generation 13, but the hope for a better tomorrow is slimmer than it was for previous generations.

(percent of children under age 18 in poverty, 1960–92)

30%

20%

10%

0%

1960   1970   1980   1992

Source: Census Bureau

more important determinant of the divorce rate than men's, because women are far more likely to initiate divorces.

Women are more favorable than men toward divorce. In a 1987 survey, women under age 25 or aged 65 and older agreed with men in their age cohorts about divorce. Boomer and pre-boomer women, however, were at odds with their male peers; they also approved of divorce more strongly than other women. In a 1992 survey, post-boomer women (aged 18 to 29) were significantly more positive about their relationships with men than were older women. Will those more positive relationships translate into a lower divorce rate in the future?

Younger women's attitudes may become more negative about divorce as they encounter the rigors of parenthood and family life. On the other hand, like women now older than age 65, post-boomer women may continue to disapprove of divorce.

As boomer and pre-boomer women age beyond the divorce-prone years, the divorce rate will depend on the attitudes of post-boomer women. With their tendencies to (a) delay marriage, (b) to cohabit instead of marry, and (c) to embrace more security-oriented attitudes, these post-boomer women may cause the divorce rate to fall. Generation 13 men will also play a deciding role. And if men and women of Generation 13 have fewer extramarital affairs, perhaps because they fear AIDS, another cause of divorce will be weakened.

Thirteeners have strong feelings about family issues, feelings that will last for decades, if not their entire lives. Security is a central issue for them. As young adults, however, they fear that security is unattainable. They struggle for security, experimenting gingerly with mating alternatives like cohabitation and delayed marriage. Some enter marriage with a clear expectation of divorce and subsequent single parenthood.

Marketers must do extensive research to turn their knowledge of social trends into concrete marketing strategy. Not all family themes are right for all generations. Post-boomers may gravitate more toward egalitarianism, with heavy doses of child protection and nurturance. Boomers may be more likely to respond positively to the trials and triumphs of parenting and caring for elderly parents. Only solid marketing research can say which themes will garner the best responses from each generation.

▶ **Boomers and Family**

Thirteeners have strong feelings about family issues. Security is a central issue for them. As young adults, however, they fear that security is unattainable. Some enter marriage with a clear expectation of divorce and subsequent single parenthood.

REFERENCES

Associated Press. "Anorexia, Bulimia Cases on the Increase in B.C." *The Seattle Times/Seattle Post-Intelligence,* March 12, 1989, p. D3.

Carey, Elaine. "Young Woman Feel Quality of Life Better than Moms Enjoyed." *Vancouver Sun,* May 25, 1992, p. A3.

Chadwick, Bruce A. and Tim B. Heaton. *Statistical Handbook of the American Family.* Phoenix, AZ: Oryx Press, 1992.

Edmondson, Brad. "Burned-out Boomers Flee to Families." *American Demographics,* December, 1991, p. 17.

Federal Council on the Aging. *Annual Report to the President, 1985.* Washington, DC: DHHS Publication No. DHDS 86-20824, p. 12.

Hardie, Ann and *Sun* staff. "In Praise of Older Parents." *The Vancouver Sun,* November 26, 1991, p. C1.

Hunter, Ski and Martin Sundel, editors. *Midlife Myths.* Newbury Park, CA: Sage Publications, 1989.

Levine, James A. "Living Together in the U.S." presentation at *Consumer Outlook XII: American Demographics' 12th Annual Conference on Consumer Trends and Markets,* June 9, 1992, New York, NY.

Levit, Katharine, Helen C. Lazenby, Cathy A. Cowan, and Suzanne W. Letsch. "National Health Expenditures, 1990." *Health Care Financing Review,* Fall 1991, Vol. 13, No. 1, pp. 29-54.

Maas, Henry. "Social Responsibility in Middle Age: Prospects and Preconditions." *Midlife Myths.* Newbury Park, CA: Sage Publications, 1989.

Mitchell, Alanna. "Suicide: A Part of Everyday Life?" *The Globe and Mail,* August 14, 1991, p. A1.

New World Decisions, Inc. *Perspectives on Middle Age:*

The Vintage Years. American Board of Family Practice: Lexington, KY, 1990.

Osius, Isobel. "A Day Late and a Dollar Short: A Portrait of Post-Boomers." *Marketing Tools Alert: A Special Supplement to American Demographics,* September 1990, pp. 4-16.

Ostroff, Jeff. "Targeting the Prime-Life Consumer." *American Demographics,* January 1991, p. 53.

Riche, Martha Farnsworth. "The Boomerang Age." *American Demographics,* May 1990, pp. 26-27.

Romaniuc, A. "Current Demographic Analysis: Fertility in Canada: From Baby Boom to Baby Bust." *Statistics Canada Catalogue 91-524E Occasional,* Ottawa, Canada: Minister of Supply and Services, 1984, pp. 22-23.

Schaie, K. Warner. "Toward a Stage Theory of Adult Cognitive Development." *Journal of Aging and Human Development, 8,* pp. 129-138.

Schaie, K. Warner and Sherry L. Willis. *Adult Development and Aging,* 2/e. Glenview, IL: Scott, Foresman & Co., 1986.

Schwartz, Joe. "Is the Baby Boomlet Ending?" *American Demographics,* May 1992, p. 9.

Scotland, Randall. "Solving Riddles of What Makes Teens Tick." *The Financial Post,* May 26, 1992, p. 15.

Shank, Susan. "Women and the Labor Market: The Link Grows Stronger." *Monthly Labor Review,* U.S. Department of Labor, March 1988, pp. 3-8.

Strauss, William and Neil Howe. *Generations: The History of America's Future, 1584 to 2069.* New York: William Morrow and Company, 1991.

Troll, Lillian E. "Myths of Midlife Intergenerational Relationships." *Midlife Myths.* Newbury Park, CA: Sage Publications, 1989.

U.S. Department of Commerce. *Statistical Abstract of the United States, 1990,* p. 87. Bureau of the Census, 1990.

Wallerstein, Judith and Sandra Blakeslee. *Second Chances: Men, Women, & Children a Decade after Divorce.* New York: Ticknor & Fields, 1989.

CHAPTER THREE

Family Economics

In 1989, the U.S. trend toward smaller households that had continued for 140 years hit bottom, at 2.62 persons per household, and stayed there through 1990 and 1991.

Smaller households are more common in individualistic and affluent cultures, among which the U.S. is preeminent. Part of the link between individualism and smaller households is that children are trained to break away from their families and strike out on their own. This was a good strategy during early-American history, when an open frontier awaited pioneers, and generation after generation exceeded the living standards of their parents.

Breaking away from the family also made sense during the industrial revolution, when parents were in the country but jobs for children were in the city. By the 1950s, the rural-to-urban migration was in full swing. City jobs paid enough for one parent to stay home with children while the other worked, which removed another reason for maintaining larger households. Sharing of child-care responsibilities among generations was no longer so necessary.

Bringing Families Closer Together Again

Generations of Americans have been raised with the expectation that their own personal futures would hold opportunities for individual autonomy and freedom, for personal fulfillment as well as a higher standard of living. The increasing affluence and personal growth opportunities that followed World War II validated these expectations for many people.

But moving away from one's parents to take a job these days is likely to provide psychological fulfillment without financial gain. The financial rewards of staying close to home are greater than before, partially because jobs are closer to where parents and their young-adult children already live.

▶**Close Families**

Families are rediscovering the financial advantages of sticking close together. With less reason for geographic separation, one of the biggest barriers to ongoing mutual influence among family members and relatives is falling.

Two changes in workplace location and scheduling contribute to this trend. First, existing manufacturing and office jobs are leaving the urban cores of major cities. At the same time, new jobs are created outside urban cores more often than before. Second, more people are working at home. As a result, fewer people have a motive for putting geographic distance between themselves and family members. With less reason for geographic separation, one of the biggest barriers to ongoing mutual influence among family members and relatives is falling.

Jobs that leave urban cores are relocating around regional suburban shopping centers or former small towns. Joel Garreau, author of *Edge City: Life on the New Frontier*, calls these centers "edge cities." Other observers have invented different names, such as "urban villages, technoburbs, suburban downtowns, suburban activity centers, major diversified centers, urban cores, galactic cities, pepperoni-pizza cities, a city of realms, superburbia, disurbs, service cities, perimeter cities, and even peripheral centers." Whatever you want to call them, people can find jobs there and afford to live close by.

Some companies are using recent advances in electronic communications to decentralize their workplaces. Satellite offices, springing up in edge cities, are in small low-rent spaces closer to where workers live. Office workers can spend most of the week at these offices, commuting to the city core once or twice a week for meetings.

Other companies have pushed the process further. AT&T wants to give each of its 10,000 account executives a "virtual office" in a laptop computer. If the plan works, executives will not need to visit an AT&T branch office, let alone an office in a city core.

Increasing numbers of people are working out of home-based offices. Laura Foote, marketing manager for Illinois Bell, says the number of Americans classified as "homeworkers" is growing at a rate of 8 percent a year. Homeworkers are adults engaged in revenue-generating or job-related work at home. Illinois Bell estimates that about 35 percent of Americans qualified as homeworkers in 1992.

People do not have to go as far as they once did to find or do work, but when they do, the job is less likely to pay enough to allow one parent to be a full-time homemaker. As a result, more people find that the financial advantages of putting distance between their parents and children are dwindling. Grandparents can help with child care, and even finances, more readily when they are close by. This may be one reason why people today are less willing to move away from family and friends for the sake of work. Since the mid-1960s, the number of Americans who have moved in the previous 12 months has declined. The only exception was when interest rates fell in 1985, and many people bought houses.

As they move around less frequently, people have more opportunity to put down roots and establish long-term relationships with those outside their household. For most people, the first circle of social relationships beyond the household is the extended family and close friends. Based on the University of Michigan's 1987-88 National Survey of Families and Households, Elizabeth Thomson and Min Li found that almost half (48 percent) of children under age 19 who were living with their mothers (and usually their fathers) have maternal grandparents within 25 miles. Three out of five children (59 percent) have maternal aunts or uncles within 25 miles. The comparable figures for children living with their fathers are 45 percent for paternal grandparents and 53 percent for paternal aunts or uncles. Even the absence of a parent does not necessarily mean less contact with grandparents or relatives. In fact, Thomson and Li found

Grandmother's House

About half of American children live within a quick drive to their grandparents, aunts, and uncles.

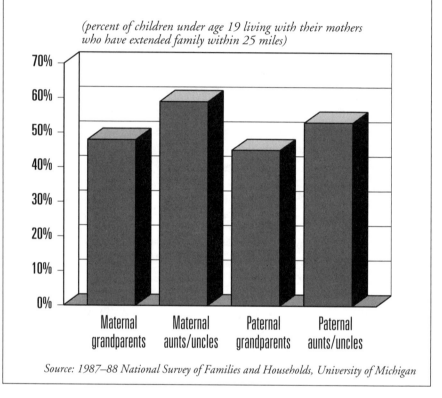

(percent of children under age 19 living with their mothers who have extended family within 25 miles)

Source: 1987–88 National Survey of Families and Households, University of Michigan

that children who lived with one parent had more contact with that parent's kin than those who lived with both parents.

Young people in particular are better off when their families of origin remain close. They are not forming new households of their own as early as previous generations did. Some demographers speculate that young adults have noticed that the price of marrying young is divorce or lost educational opportunity, and consequently lower earning power.

For most young people, higher education often means sacrificing income-earning opportunities in the short term. This, in turn, means relying on parents during the educational years. A survey of 1,500 Canadian organizations in 1991 found that half of the new jobs created during the 1990s will require at least 17 years of schooling. This means that the average young person will have to stay in school continuously and successfully up to the age of 22 to have only an even chance of getting one of those new jobs. But age 22 assumes a full courseload every year, while the trend is toward taking longer to finish degrees, which in turn means relying on parents even longer.

The Economic Pros and Cons of Family Life

Young people are not only living longer with their parents, they are also returning to the parental home more often. The child nearly always benefits from this arrangement, financially, at least; sometimes the entire household does. In one sample, about one-third of young adults who lived with their parents contributed at least part of their income to household expenses. Whether contributing or not, young adults enjoy a material advantage in remaining part of a family instead of going it alone.

Families whose financial standing deteriorated during the 1980s most often contained an older male worker who lost a job. This factor increases family members' dependence on one another. The U.S. Census Bureau recently reported a growing share of the population below the poverty line, from 13 percent in 1989 to 14 percent in 1991.

Meanwhile, the rich got relatively richer. In the mid-1960s, the wealthiest 20 percent of households had an average income only 6.1 times higher than those at the poverty line. In 1991, it was 8.4 times higher, according to Census Bureau economists. Those who improved their financial standing during the 1980s were

▶ **The Full Nest Syndrome**

Today's young adults are enjoying the material benefits of living with their parents longer than they used to.

▶ Stagnating Income?

Household incomes would have fallen even more than they did if so many women had not entered the work force during the 1980s. Now that the women who wanted and found jobs are working, there is less room for further growth in household income.

often highly educated. The end result has been a shrinking middle class.

Inflation-adjusted household incomes would have fallen even more than they did if so many women had not entered the work force during the 1980s. The decline in personal income has been masked by the increase in the number of people working in each household. When wives and mothers enter the work force, household income increases while individual incomes stand still or fall. Unlike a decade ago, however, today's families no longer have spare potential income-earners to make up financial shortfalls. Now that the women who wanted and found jobs are working, there is less room for further growth in household income.

Assuming that people would rather see their income rise than stand still or drop, members of the average household will be collectively motivated to avoid the loss of, and promote the addition of, earners. This will motivate spouses to avoid divorce and parents and children to live together longer. If families that stick together see financial advantages compared with the alternatives, the converse is also true: families that split up will be more likely to experience poverty.

Single Parents, Divorce, and Family Support

In the last 20 years, the nuclear family has given way to the single-parent family. Married couples with children have decreased as a share of all households, while all other types of households have increased. The National Center for Health Statistics (NCHS) estimates that about three in five American children (61 percent) lived with both biological parents in 1988. Since a second marriage can turn a single-parent family into a two-parent family overnight, the

NCHS estimates that almost half of American children "will live in a single-parent family *at some point* during their childhood."

Single-parent families are most likely to live in poverty. About one-third of single mothers in the U.S. live below the poverty line. Noncustodial parents are not necessarily much better off. If they live alone, they may find it expensive.

Not only do singles and single-parent families find it harder to get ahead, they also find it harder to keep from falling behind. The changing job market is making continuous, lifelong education a prerequisite to maintain a stable standard of living. A U.S. Census Bureau study reports that 75 percent of college students came straight from high school in the 1970s. By 1989, this figure was 60 percent and falling. Without a spouse to make money while they go to school, however, singles and single parents cannot make the short-term sacrifices they need to assure a better future.

Single parents who do not remarry often turn to their own parents for support. In fact, the financial pressures are such that increasing numbers of dual-parent families must look to their parents for help, too. Grandparents do more than babysit. They buy grandchildren's clothes and toys. And so many parents are helping adult children buy homes that it spurred Merrill Lynch to develop the Parent Power program. This program lets parents provide the equivalent of a down-payment for their children without drawing down their brokerage accounts and paying capital gains taxes.

For many adult Americans, having to turn to their parents for money is an admission of financial failure. In other cultures, however, cooperative family financing of real-estate holdings is a cause for pride. In Japan, Nippon Housing Loan

> ▶ **Falling Behind**
>
> The changing job market is making continuous, lifelong education a prerequisite to maintain a stable standard of living. Without a spouse to make money while they go to school, however, singles and single parents cannot make the short-term sacrifices they need to assure a better future.

Company now offers a 100-year mortgage repayable over three, or even four, generations. Borrowers can choose to pay interest only for three generations and then sell the land to pay off the principal. The loan is not available to single people. Americans may never be as family oriented as Asians. By the same token, they are unlikely to be as financially independent from their parents as they have been for the past 40 years.

▶ Will Divorce Decline?

Rising wages in industrialized countries contributed to rising divorce rates during the 20th century. The reverse may also turn out to be true. The greater risk of poverty associated with having only one earner may make people think twice about divorce.

While single parenthood has been on the rise, one of its causes, divorce, has been slackening. Throughout the 1980s, the U.S. divorce rate declined slightly. In Canada, it fell 4.5 percent from 1989 to 1990. Two major factors that could explain this phenomenon are eroded buying power and the aging of the population.

While everyone hopes buying power will improve, it is clear that the population will continue to age. That means less growth in the divorce rate, perhaps even a decline. Consequently, the economic forces driving families closer together will gain more momentum.

The older people get, the less likely they are to divorce. A 30-year-old husband in Canada has a one in three chance of being divorced by age 80. For a 50-year-old husband, the chances are only one in ten.

Many benefits of divorce may lose their potency with older people. The need to find one's own identity is more likely to have been satisfied, the need for sexual variety may subside, and the ability to tolerate annoying quirks in one's spouse may improve as middle age brings an increased awareness of one's own shortcomings.

At the same time, many costs of divorce may rise with age. One is no longer as desirable as a marriage partner, and the market of potential mates becomes smaller. Also, the need to keep the family together gains importance as old age approaches. The prospect of being a dependent in one's declining years is more bearable within the context of an intact family.

Because of stagnant or declining individual incomes, young and old alike face higher relative costs in setting up a household today than they did 15 years ago. Dr. Gary Becker, the University of Chicago-based 1992 Nobel Prize winner for economics, demonstrated that rising wages in industrialized countries contributed to rising divorce rates during the 20th century. The reverse may also turn out to be true. The greater risk of poverty associated with having only one earner may make people think twice about divorce.

Where housing is scarce and expensive, divorced couples even continue living together for months after their divorce. As low interest rates and house prices allow more renters to become homeowners, divorcees will find more rental accommodations available. But in a poor economy, going it alone looks scarier than ever from a financial point of view.

Most cultures in the world are older than that of the U.S. They have been through more periods of expansion and contraction, ascendancy and decline. As a result, they are seasoned, more resilient to the buffets of history and economics. They place more value on the family as an economic unit than does the domestic culture of the U.S.

The post-World War II era left the U.S. in economic ascendancy. With the end of the Cold War, that era has come to a close. Americans' domestic culture will mature and develop the same wisdom that is embedded in older cultures. In doing so, it will place more emphasis on the family as a financial unit.

In the consumer marketplace, the greater emphasis on the family will mean more buying decisions will be made with input from family members. As people have more contact with extended-family members, they are likely to make purchase decisions with input or influence from relatives. With the shifting patterns of job location and scheduling, and with decreasing residential mobility, young adults and young parents are more likely to influence, and be influenced by, their own empty-nester parents. Marketers who take account of those influences will be able to develop more effective marketing strategies.

Becker, Gary S. *A Treatise on the Family,* Enlarged Edition. Cambridge, MA: Harvard University Press, 1991.

British Columbia Report, April 20, 1992, p. 19.

Celente, Gerald, and Tom Milton. *Trend Tracking.* New York: John Wiley & Sons, 1990.

Dawson, Deborah, A. *1988 Health Interview Survey on Child Health.* Hyattsville, MD: National Center for Health Statisitics, 1988.

Francese, Peter. "The Dream Is Aging." *American Demographics,* March 1992, p. 2.

Garreau, Joel. *Edge City: Life on the New Frontier.* New York: Doubleday, 1991.

Hofstede, G. "Dimensions of National Cultures in Fifty Countries and Three Regions." *Expiscations in Cross-Cultural Psychology.* Deregowski, J.B., Dziurawiec, S., and Annis, R.C., editors. Lisse, The Netherlands: Swets & Zeitinger B.V., 1983, pp. 335-355.

Hudson Institute of Canada and Towers Perrin. *Workforce 2000: Competing in a Seller's Market: Is Canadian Management Prepared?* Toronto, ON: The Hudson Institute of Canada and Towers Perrin, 1991.

"Kids' Contact with Kith and Kin." *The Numbers News,* June 1992, p. 6.

Long, Larry. "Americans on the Move." *American Demographics,* June 1990, p. 48.

Riche, Martha Farnsworth. "The Boomerang Age." *American Demographics,* May 1990, pp. 26-27.

Sauvé, Roger. *Canadian People Patterns.* Saskatoon, Saskatchewan: Western Producer Prairie Books, 1990, p. 42, 46.

Schlossberg, Howard. "Illinois Bell Predicts More Americans Will Start Doing their Homework." *Market-*

REFERENCES

REFERENCES

ing News, September 16, 1992, p. 10. (Published by American Marketing Association, Chicago, IL.)

Taylor, Thayer. "Back to the Future." *Marketing Executive Report*, 2 (August 1992), pp. 1, 10-13. (published by American Marketing Association, Chicago, IL.)

Thomson, Robert. "The 100-Year Mortgage Hits Japan." *The Financial Post*, January 31, 1990, p. 9.

U.S. Bureau of the Census. "Household and Family Characteristics: March 1990 and 1989." *Current Population Reports*, Series P-20, No. 447, 1990.

U.S. Bureau of the Census. "School Enrollment: Social and Economic Characteristics of Students: October 1989." *Current Population Reports*, Series P-20, No. 452, 1989.

Waggoner, John. "Parents Pledge Assets to Help Kids Buy Homes." *USA Today*, March 27, 1992, p. 1B.

CHAPTER FOUR

Families and Popular Culture

People are shocked and alarmed by the statistics on family fragmentation. "Save the Family" has replaced "Save the Whales." A broad range of social trends are converging to intensify the focus on the family and its social value. Popular trends, political campaigns, buzzwords, movements, TV shows, movies, and magazines help to reemphasize the importance of family.

All of us have our own vision of what the family "should" look like. Some see diversity as the ideal: others would like to emulate the Andersons from the 1950s TV series "Father Knows Best." One thing everyone will agree on in the coming years is that the well-being of families is essential to the prosperity of the neighborhood, the community, and the nation. As a result, different visions of the ideal family will vie for the right to be the accepted cultural norm and the basis for public policy.

Marketers who want to take a family marketing approach must stay abreast of the public debate over what constitutes an optimally functional family. Specific target markets may sit on different sides of the political fence. At the same time, vast areas of common ground resonate with people of all political persuasions.

We can't ignore the political dimensions of family issues. In the

1992 U.S. presidential election, the Republicans noticed that beliefs, attitudes, and values related to family issues were changing. They latched onto this trend and tried, unsuccessfully, to turn it to their advantage. Why did they mistakenly think the trend was their friend?

They realized that while they were in control of the government, liberals had taken control of the social issues related to family. In fact, disparate interest groups, united by little more than their postmodernist critique of Cold War thinking, had owned family, children's, and women's issues for almost a quarter of a century. From 1981 to 1988, public opinion became more liberal on issues like the role and status of women, education, racial equality, and health care. Republican strategists apparently guessed that a shift away from liberal thinking on family issues meant a shift toward Pat Robertson-style moralizing across the board. They were wrong. Instead, a third option was emerging.

A Neotraditional Synthesis

This third option might best be described as a shift toward "neotraditional" values. The term "neotraditional" reminds us that a synthesis of values has occurred. We have not gone backwards, but neither have we rejected the wisdom of the past. In a 1992 article in *Psychology Today,* psychologist William Doherty speaks of the neotraditional family as an advancement beyond the postmodern family. Marilyn Sandler, president of the Creative Research Group in Toronto, identifies "neotraditional" values that consumers of the 1990s will use in marketplace decisionmaking. The value shifts she describes manifest a deeper level of social change and accompany shifts in interpersonal relationships and social roles in the most fundamental unit of society, the family. The influx of women into the work force has made the full-time homemaker a rarity in families with children at home. Families in which all the children are school-aged are especially unlikely to include a full-time homemaker.

When women become paid workers, they increase their financial power within the family and reduce the time they have available for housework. As a result, neotraditional families do not typically distribute homemaking responsibilities strictly by gender. Instead, they distribute them through negotiation and mutual consent. Who does what is often less important than how the decision was made.

Traditional and modern families assigned tasks more on the basis of gender. Even the postmodern family uses gender as a basis for task distribution, although the guiding principle is role-reversal. The postmodern woman feels she must be a breadwinner and feels humiliated or oppressed by housework. The neotraditional woman, by contrast, negotiates to do what she enjoys, even if some of the tasks she likes happen to be traditional female tasks.

Neotraditional fathers do not view themselves as sole breadwinners and, consequently, don't see their wives as having sole responsibility for the children. They want more time with their children and reject any advertising or ideology that portrays child care or family concerns as women's exclusive turf. They are equally turned off by anything that glorifies workaholism for fathers.

The central value of neotraditional thinking may be child protection. Neotraditionalists actively support the elimination of child abuse. Reacting to the tendency for *laissez faire* child-rearing in the postmodern family, neotraditionalists reemphasize the importance of parental authority. They believe that without clear limits, children become insecure and fail to learn self-control. This trend stands out most clearly in the area of teen sexuality. The threat of AIDS puts teens in a kind of danger unknown since before the discovery of antibiotics for the treatment of sexually transmitted diseases.

In traditional families, disaffected couples stay together unhappily "for the sake of the children." They see monogamy as a moral obligation. Postmodern couples, by contrast, might divorce as soon as the excitement of the honeymoon begins to fade. They see life-long monogamy as just one of many equally valid lifestyle choices.

> ▶ **Looking Backward**
>
> The term neotraditional reminds us that a synthesis of values has occurred. We have not gone backwards, but neither have we rejected the wisdom of the past.

Neotraditionalists reject both attitudes. They see marital difficulties as a challenge to personal growth, and when relationship problems arise, they seek counseling not a different relationship. Knowing that all hatred is self-hatred, they work toward self-acceptance as a path to mutual acceptance and will not stay together under any and all circumstances. They will, however, accept a fundamental change in their personalities as a fair price for a successful marriage.

These changes in perspective point to a groping effort to reconstruct social roles and expectations. Neotraditionalists are reinventing the family to suit more diverse life circumstances, at the same time that they take account of unchanging human needs, especially those of children. This change creates conflict for those who either do not want to change or want to change in a different direction. If these traditional or postmodern opponents of neotraditionalism are your customers, you will need to know how they are reacting and feeling.

Today, self-interested individualists are more likely to be pilloried than admired. James Stewart's investigative book *Den of Thieves* documents the egocentrism of investment hot-shots like Ivan Boesky and Michael Milken. Tom Wolfe's bestselling novel *Bonfire of the Vanities* scorned the "me first," "everyone for himself" attitudes of 1980s' Wall Street manipulators. Its popularity led to a movie.

Scrambling for career success is not only selfish; it cuts into family time. The competition is always stiffer for the next rung on the corporate ladder or the next badge of business achievement. Older boomers, men and women alike, are hitting a bottleneck between middle management and upper manage-

> ▶ **Know Your Customers**
>
> Neotraditionalists are reinventing the family to suit more diverse life circumstances, at the same time that they take account of unchanging human needs, especially those of children. If your customers are traditional or postmodern opponents of neotraditionalism, you need to know how they are reacting and feeling.

ment. When people hit the career ceiling, they typically shift their energy from work toward family. In 1990, *GQ* magazine commissioned a survey of over 1,200 American men. Compared with only two years earlier, 11 percent more said that family was the most important part of their lives. In a survey conducted by Louis Harris and Associates for *Men's Health* magazine, 48 percent responded that a happy family was essential, while only 26 percent said that career success was essential.

The 1992 hit movie *The Mighty Ducks* highlighted these shifting priorities. The hero, a workaholic cutthroat lawyer, valued winning above all else. By the end of the movie, his community service work led him to the threshold of a new job, a home life, and a father-son relationship. In other words, he rejected the 1980s and accepted the 1990s.

In another rejection of the materialistic 1980s, consumers today are more interested in reducing their debt load than in acquiring more possessions. This is a part of what has been called the "back-to-basics" movement, and it extends to cultural interests. For instance, a broad base of consumers pay more attention to down-home images like those associated with country music. Hip new country stars draw a more mainstream audience, which has made advertisers more interested in The Nashville Network and Country Music Television.

Even the wealthy are affected by the revolt against 1980s' excesses. According to Jane Fitzgibbon of the TrendSights division of Ogilvy and Mather, the wealthy have toned down their consumption. Things that scream money, glamour, and glitz have been replaced by "stealth wealth," a quiet, understated emphasis on quality.

Making heaps of money is secondary for those who put more emphasis on family. Nancy Langton, a professor at the University of British Columbia, conducted a survey of 980 Stanford MBAs. She found that those who rated family life as more important earned less, and they were less likely to be on the fast track to the CEO suite. Langton notes that their willingness to make career sacrifices testifies to the importance of family time even among high-level workers.

Not everyone is thrilled about the back-to-basics trend. Those who have "made it" and moved upscale are still looking for unique, high-quality and, inevitably, expensive items. One upscale fashion manufacturer, Charivari Ltd., got a strong response to billboard ads that read, "Ripped Jeans. Pocket Tees. Back to Basics. *Wake us when it's over.*" If the economy improves and prosperity is widespread, we could see a return to the pursuit of possessions.

Neotraditionalism and Gender Roles

The growing numbers of dual-income and single-parent families are delegating and simplifying household management tasks. They are time poor, especially working mothers. As a result, the neotraditional family includes a variety of new decision makers, buyers, and users of household products and services.

As their parents cope with the time crunch, many teenagers in dual-income and single-parent families take an active role in household shopping. The small size of today's teen cohort obscures the momentous change taking place in teen consumer behavior. While young adults may have to delay independent living because of financial constraints, they are learning to shop for the family sooner because of their parents' time constraints.

In a survey of 21,000 employees in 400 cities and towns across Canada, Linda Duxbury of Carleton University, Ottawa, found 70 percent wanted to end the nine-to-five, Monday-through-Friday workweeks, so they could better meet family commitments.

Yankelovich Partners has found much the same in its environmental attitude scans. Throughout the 1980s, surveys showed a steady rise in women's interest in work. In 1987, only 35 percent of women said they would stop working if they suddenly had enough money. In 1990, however, 56 percent felt this way. The percentage endorsing part-time work as the best arrangement for mothers rose rapidly, while the group that wanted a full-time career fell to its smallest size in 20 years. Observers like Marilyn Sandler say that because so many women now know what working is really like, they are less likely to see it as a path to fulfillment. Like men, they are now more likely to work just for the money.

Many newspaper and magazine articles have commented on women's increasing disenchantment with careers. Some articles have prompted a backlash from those who do not want to believe the message. In February 1992, *Chatelaine*, a Canadian women's magazine, published an article in which full-time homemakers discussed the positive aspects of their work and the lack of respect they sometimes get from career women. The article set off a backlash of criticism from feminist journalists and politicians, who repeatedly raised the specter of a return to 1950s-style gender roles in which women had no options other than homemaking. Critics also lament the guilt that pro-homemaking, "momist" articles induce in working women.

Marketers targeting women sympathetic to the backlash must take account of feminists' fears. Their fear of a return to "domestic servitude" assumes that most men still have the earning power to support an entire family on a single income. Unrealistic as that assumption may be, it still colors feminists' perceptions of the world, including their perceptions of advertisements. They are repelled by images of female homemakers. Feminists, as well as other working women, may respond favorably to advertising messages that emphasize the personal fulfillment that comes from working outside the home.

As women continue to sort through the work-family conflict, the men's movement has begun to exalt fatherhood over bachelorhood and the macho ethos of the strong, silent man. Advertisements showing men with babies quickly became a cliché in the early 1990s, selling everything from Ivory soap to Toyotas. Behind the schmaltz, however, is a fundamental change in the masculine ideal. American men play many roles in their lives. The importance of some of these roles has recently declined, while that of others has increased.

The soldier role is less important now. Cuts in military bud-

> ## ▶ Materialism Is Out
>
> Consumers today are more interested in reducing their debt load than in acquiring more possessions. This is a part of what has been called the "back-to-basics" movement, and it extends to cultural interests.

gets have greatly reduced the number of people on military and defense industry payrolls. The military establishment has fired admirals for macho, sexist handling of sexual-harassment complaints. Popeye and Brutus have been replaced by Teddy Ruxpin and the Care Bears, and war toys are seen as symptoms of parental ignorance or neglect.

▶ The New Man

As women continue to sort through the work-family conflict, the men's movement has begun to exalt fatherhood over bachelorhood and the macho ethos of the strong, silent man.

The father role is now more important, which isn't necessarily saying much. Historically, men's roles as fathers have ranked near the bottom in importance, compared with their other roles. Even as recently as the mid-1970s, women and men alike viewed men's parenting abilities with skepticism. In 1978, one scholar reviewed the scientific literature on fathering and discovered a new perspective, the notion that men have the *ability* "to participate in the full range of parenting behaviors."

One social scientist of the mid-1970s summed up the attitude of the day with the stunning statement that "the role requirements of having a career and being a good father are not contradictory." Although this attitude sounds archaic today, remember that in the late 1960s and early 1970s, people in the young-family stage of the lifecycle were members of what Strauss and Howe call "the Silent Generation." They were the last generation to live in traditional nuclear families with a male breadwinner and a female full-time homemaker.

Today, television shows like "Cosby" and "Roseanne" deal with fatherhood realistically. But popular culture also manifests a more ambiguous attitude for men. The movie *Three Men and a Baby* laughed at men playing the parental role. *Ghost Dad* showed a competent, concerned father but could not quite bring itself to present him as a real-live person. In another pro-fatherhood movie, *Men Don't Leave*, Dad was killed off in the first 15 minutes.

Popular culture's ambivalence toward positive depictions of fatherhood reflects ambivalence among consumers. Pro-fatherhood messages and images can stir rejection by some consumer segments, particularly among people who equate fatherhood with child abuse, authoritarian patriarchy, and child abandonment. Marketers may be able to tap these people's buried yearning for unfulfilled experiences of positive father-child relationships, but they will have to do careful research to create ads that maneuver past the negative stereotypes.

> ▶ **Daddy Dearest**
>
> Not everyone has a positive image of fatherhood. Marketers have to be careful in their approach to those who have bad memories of abuse and authoritarianism.

Pregnancy has some negative stereotypes, too. In the 1970s and 1980s, the media had plenty to say about pregnancy, especially if it was unplanned or happened to teenagers. It was responsible for arrested educational and career opportunities. It became the focus of women's struggle to have their special needs recognized in a male-dominated medical system. It was even a symbol of patriarchal oppression in a system that prevented women from getting abortions on demand.

It is still all of those things for many people. Increasingly, however, popular culture lets through a few faint rays of sunnier attitudes toward pregnancy. Mattel has developed My Bundle Baby, a strap-on abdomen that simulates some aspects of pregnancy. The pouch kicks like a real fetus and produces an audible heartbeat. Hasbro's Puppy Surprise, a plush mother dog with three or four puppies inside, is selling well. The Mommy-To-Be doll, imported from Scandinavia by Judith Corp., has a removable abdomen cover with a baby inside. Although the doll has been condemned as unrealistic because it returns to a slim figure immediately after childbirth, sales are good.

The cover of the August 1991 issue of *Vanity Fair* showed actress Demi Moore nude and pregnant. Reactions on both sides were extreme. Champions of decency had it removed from supermarket shelves, while journalists quoted people waxing lyrical about the beauty of pregnancy.

Obviously, the various segments of society have different feelings about pregnancy and childbirth. What's new, however, is the greater diversity of feelings being expressed today. We have come to an end of an era in which positive feelings about pregnancy were virtually absent from popular culture.

Parents and Children

Today's baby-boom parents are better educated than their mothers were, and they respond well to instructive material on parenting. YTV, a youth-oriented Canadian cable channel, has developed a program called "Positive Parenting." The show deliberately targets boomer parents with information and advice on everything from discipline to money sense to sexuality. Host Debbie Van Kiekebelt says of boomer parents like herself, "We're a generation that really cares about learning to become better parents, even though our own parents may laugh at us, with all our books and experts."

Baby-boom parents are also older parents. The dramatic increase over the past 15 years in the number of women who have their *first* child after the age of 30 may ultimately reduce the share of childless-couple households. The increase in the number of second marriages has also contributed to the trend toward older parents of newborns. Older parents say they no longer care so much about financial and career success but are looking for the more substantial emotional rewards that parenthood can bring.

The growing interest in parenting skills parallels a decreasing tolerance for child abuse and neglect. In 1992, Gregory Kingsley of Florida "divorced" his mother. This was the first case of its kind but probably not the last. The children's rights movement has been gathering steam and is starting to win some legal battles.

In September 1992, three U.S. television networks recognized the growing public interest in child-protection issues and cooperated in simultaneously airing a special on child abuse. The special, entitled "Scared Silent," was produced by Arnold Shapiro and featured TV talk-show star Oprah Winfrey as host. The audience was massive. Likewise, one of the best-selling self-help books in the past ten years, *The Courage to Heal* by Ellen Bass and Laura Davis, deals with recovery from childhood sexual abuse.

The growing emphasis on protecting children also affects teenagers, who face dangers related to drug use and sexual activity. Postmodernists reject socially imposed moral dictums in favor of individually chosen ethical standards, even when the individual is young and impressionable. They promote the distribution of condoms and education about safe sexual practices. Traditionalists, by contrast, see AIDS as a vindication of the moral high ground associated with chastity, and promote sexual abstinence for unmarried persons. Taking the middle ground, neotraditionalists see practical benefits in some traditional taboos. They realize that child-rearing for teens typically supresses educational attainment. Therefore, they encourage teens to delay pregnancy, either through abstinence or safe sex.

> ▶ **New-Wave Parents**
>
> Baby boomers are better educated than their parents. They are also starting families at later ages. As a result, they seek out parenting information and espouse children's rights.

Traditionalists and neotraditionalists together are having an impact on teen culture. TV shows like "Life Goes On" and "Beverly Hills 90210" provide role models for abstinence. One study shows that the proportion of 26-year-old women who were virgins increased from about 5 percent in 1982 to about 10 percent in 1988. Although the share of teen virgins has not increased, the trend may eventually spread to younger ages. Changes in social attitudes toward sexual mores can precede changes in sexual behavior by several years. Sociologists David Reed and Martin Weinberg, in their 1984 article in *Social Psychology Quarterly*, found a lag between changes in sexual attitudes that took place in the 1960s and corresponding changes in behavior that did not appear until the 1970s. If Reed and Weinberg are right, the 1990s may usher in a more studious, less sexual, teen culture.

Monogamy and Long-Term Commitments

Any given target market segment has a unique mix of traditional marriages, postmodern "relationships," and neotraditional marriages. Each type has its own attitude toward commitment.

In traditional marriages, couples stay together despite problems. If they have an unhappy marriage, their commitment to being a "good husband" or a "good wife" makes divorce too emotionally distasteful. If they seek psychological or sexual fulfillment, they do so covertly. Dalma Heyn's 1992 book *The Erotic Silence of the American Wife* describes women so enslaved by their own "good wife" ideals that they cannot openly seek sexual excitement with their own husbands, but instead turn to covert affairs. Some chocolate manufacturers have used this emotional complex in ads that draw an analogy between covertly enjoying chocolate and covertly enjoying sex.

The Woody Allen/Mia Farrow scandal made headlines in the midst of the "family values" debate of the 1992 U.S. presidential election campaign. Woody and Mia are the epitome of the postmodern family. They are not married, have children together, but do not live together.

Twenty years ago, when postmodernism was in its heyday, Woody and Mia's relationship would have been admired as an example of liberated enlightenment. In 1975, one of the best-selling books on relationships was *Open Marriage: A New Lifestyle for Couples,* by George and Nena O'Neill. The book counseled married couples on the advantages of generously accepting their partner's needs for intimate relationships with multiple others, not excluding extramarital sexual relationships. The book set the moral standard for baby boomers, who were then entering the mate-selection stage.

Nena O'Neill has since condemned the ideas presented in *Open Marriage.* No doubt, many baby boomers who bought the philosophy in the 1970s have rejected it too. Woody and Mia's relationship is no longer regarded as the kind of ideal young people should strive for. Nonetheless, postmodernists still exist. For some marketers, they may represent a valuable target segment. Product positioning emotionally connected to independence, having-it-all, or the validation of alternative relationship styles could appeal to them.

Today's marriage gurus are chanting a different mantra from the O'Neills. Instead of running away from marital difficulties and dissatisfactions, they advocate facing them head-on. John Bradshaw, a popular author and speaker on family dysfunctionality, promotes emotionally working through the dysfunction in one's family of origin to see how it crops up in current family relationships.

Some companies offer employees free or subsidized psychological counseling. The kinds of problems counselors used to see most often were drug- and alcohol-related. Recently, however, they are seeing more family-related issues, according to Melanie Bot, a senior human resources consultant at Peat, Marwick, Stevenson & Kellogg in Toronto. Neotraditionalists will respond well to advertising messages linked to feelings of being supported emotionally while resolving differences, maintaining loyalty through adversity, and accepting personal change gracefully.

The increasing importance of family is not just reflected in the media but also in corporate budgets. Buzzwords like "flextime," "the mommy-and-daddy track," and "the electronic cottage," show that employers are recognizing the importance of the family in attracting, keeping, and motivating employees. To satisfy the demand for more family time, some employers are creating more family-friendly options, such as working at home. Illinois Bell found that 31 percent of Americans were "homeworkers" in 1990. Homeworkers were defined as people aged 18 and older who generate revenue or do job-related work at home. They also found that the homeworker market was growing at an incredible rate of 8 percent each year. Likewise, Allan Cohen and Associates of Richmond Hill, Ontario, predicts that by the year 2000, 40 percent of Canadians will work at home at least some of the time. Many will be self-employed. Because self-employment often allows one to work at home, more people are expected to choose it over continuing in a stalled climb up the corporate ladder.

> ▶ **New-Age Kids**
>
> Just as parents are different today, so are kids. The 1990s may usher in a more studious, less sexual, teen culture.

Family Benefits in Medium and Large Firms

Corporations are recognizing that family-friendly benefits and policies are important in attracting and keeping good employees.

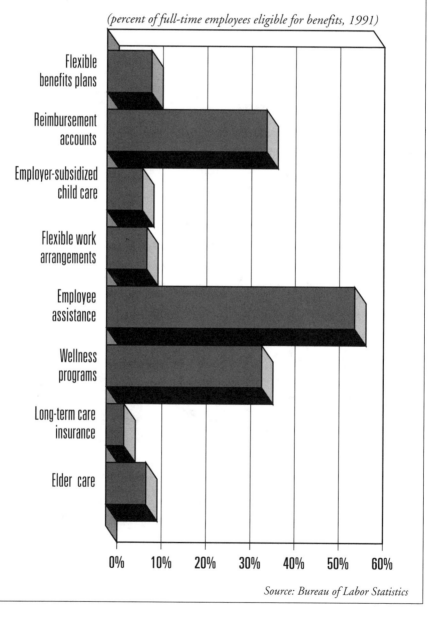

(percent of full-time employees eligible for benefits, 1991)

Flexible benefits plans

Reimbursement accounts

Employer-subsidized child care

Flexible work arrangements

Employee assistance

Wellness programs

Long-term care insurance

Elder care

0%   10%   20%   30%   40%   50%   60%

Source: Bureau of Labor Statistics

The New York City-based Families and Work Institute recently published a report card on how well U.S. corporations are doing with "family-friendly" programs such as flexible schedules, job sharing, and child-care assistance. It notes that, although a decade ago such programs did not exist, today all large employers offer some. Likewise, a Conference Board survey of 521 senior human-resources executives in the largest U.S. corporations found a trend toward more flextime. Programs related to employees' child care and elder care needs are the fastest-growing corporate benefits, according to those executives who predict more alternative work arrangements in the future. These include job sharing, phased retirement, and home-based work.

Popular culture sends out varied and sometimes contradictory messages about "the family." To some extent, these varied views reflect the diversity of views in the general population. Some segments of the market espouse the modern family as the ideal. Other segments see greater benefits in the postmodern family form. More recently, popular culture seems to be pointing toward a third ideal, the neotraditional family. To develop strategies in tune with the way customers think about the family, marketers need to know which views are rising or falling in popularity. The growing popularity of neotraditional attitudes is reflected in politics, polls, books of fiction, self-help trends, TV shows, advertising, toy fads, and trends in human-resource management.

REFERENCES

Barsky, Lesley. "Our Families Come First: Why More Mothers are Choosing to Stay Home." *Chatelaine*, February 1992, p. 49.

Bass, Ellen, and Laura Davis. *The Courage to Heal.* New York: Harper & Row, 1988.

Bradshaw, John. *Homecoming: Reclaiming and Championing Your Inner Child.* New York: Bantam Books, 1990.

Bradshaw, John. *On the Family: A Revolutionary Way of Self-Discovery.* Deerfield Beach, FL: Health Communications, Inc., 1988.

REFERENCES

Braverman, Michael. *Life Goes On.* Beverly Hills, CA: FOX, 1990.

Brickman, Paul. *Men Don't Leave.* New York, NY: Warner Bros., 1990.

Canadian Press. "Media Momism Mode Miffs Working Moms." *The Vancouver Sun,* April 28, 1992, p. C2.

Carsey-Werner Co. in association with Bill Cosby. *The Cosby Show.* New York, NY: NBC, 1984.

Conference Board, cited in "Forecasters' Talk." *Credit Union News,* January 25, 1990, p. 22.

Darley, Susan A. "Big Time Careers for the Little Woman: A Dual-Role Dilemma." *Journal of Social Issues,* Vol. 32, No. 3, 1976, pp. 85-98.

Doherty, William J. "Private Lives, Public Values: The New Pluralism—A Report from the Heartland." *Psychology Today,* Vol. 25, No. 3, May/June 1992, pp. 33-37, 82.

Downey, Maureen. "Babes in Toyland Wombs Stir Debate over Family Values." *The Vancouver Sun,* July 13, 1992, p. C1.

"Even More About Nude Demi Moore." *The Vancouver Sun,* July 19, 1991, p. C8.

Fein, Robert A. "Research on Fathering: Social Policy and an Emergent Perspective." *Journal of Social Issues, 34,* 1, 1978, pp. 122-135.

Fitzgibbon, Jane. Quoted by Michelle Osborn. "Conspicuous Consumption is Déclassé." *USA Today,* November 29, 1991, p. 1A.

Goerne, Carrie. "Consumers Bored by the '90s Yearn for Finer Things in Life." *Marketing News,* June 8, 1992, p. 23.

Goerne, Carrie. "The Nation Goes Country." *Marketing News,* April 13, 1992, p. 1.

REFERENCES

Herek, Stephen. *The Mighty Ducks*. Burbank, CA: Buena Vista, 1992.

Heyn, Dalma. *The Erotic Silence of the American Wife*. New York: Random House/Turtle Bay Books, 1992.

Hogarth, Don. "Don't Forget Home Work." *The Financial Post*, September 24, 1991, p. 15.

Katzman, Leonard, and Larry Hagman. *Dallas*. Burbank, CA: CBS, 1978.

Lawlor, Julia. "Companies Get C for Sensitivity." *USA Today*, November 15, 1991, p. 1B.

Mayer, William G. "The Shifting Sands of Public Opinion: Is Liberalism Back?" *The Public Interest*, Spring 1992, pp. 3-16.

Mishima, Carrie. "All Work, No Play... " *The Vancouver Sun*, December 7, 1991, p. C1.

Nimoy, Leonard. *Three Men and a Baby*. Burbank, CA: Buena Vista, 1987.

O'Neill, George and Nena O'Neill. *Open Marriage: A New Lifestyle for Couples*. New York: Evans, M., and Co., 1975.

Peterson, Karen S. "Virginity May Be Gaining a New Cachet." *USA Today*, July 24, 1992, p. 2D.

Piirto, Rebecca. "New Women's Revolution." *American Demographics*, April 1991, p. 6.

Poitier, Sydney. *Ghost Dad*. Universal City, CA: Universal, 1990.

Prokaska, Lee. "Today's Parents and Children." *TV Times*, August 10, 1990, p. 32.

"Public Servants Earn More, Are Absent More." *The Financial Post*, April 27, 1992, p. 3.

Ramsay, Laura. "Firms Beef Up Staff Support Systems." *The Financial Post*, September 25, 1991, p. 35.

REFERENCES

Reed, David, and Martin S. Weinberg. "Premarital Coitus: Developing and Established Sexual Scripts." *Social Psychology Quarterly, 47,* 2, 1984, pp. 129-138.

Rosin, Charles. *Beverly Hills 90210.* Beverly Hills, CA: FOX, 1990.

Russell, William and Peter Tewksbury. *Father Knows Best.* Burbank, CA: CBS, 1954.

Sandler, Marilyn. "The Consumer of the '90s." *Marketline,* September 1990, p. 4.

Sandler, Marilyn. "The Consumer of the '90s." *Marketline,* November 1990, p. 4.

Schlossberg, Howard. "Illinois Bell Predicts More Americans Will Start Doing Their Homework." *Marketing News,* September 16, 1992, p. 10.

Schwartz, Joe. "New Priorities." *American Demographics,* October 1990, p. 13.

Smith, David. "Women in Workforce on Threshold of Major Changes, Seminar Told." *The Vancouver Sun,* May 7, 1992, p. D3.

Stewart, James B. *Den of Thieves.* New York: Simon & Schuster, 1991.

U.S. Department of Health and Human Services. *National Survey of Family Growth, 1982-1988.* Hyattsville, MD: Public Health Service, Center for Disease Control, National Center for Health Statististics.

Werner, Tom, Carsey Marcy, Jay Daniel, and Bob Myer. *Roseanne.* Burbank, CA: ABC, 1988.

Wolfe, Tom. *Bonfire of the Vanities.* New York: Bantam, 1988.

CHAPTER FIVE

New American Families

The Disney animated movie *An American Tail* opens with mice coming to the United States aboard a ship carrying human immigrants from Europe. It is based on the popular image of huddled masses streaming past the Statue of Liberty as they flee the repression of the old world for the freedom of the new. This image can cost you money if you mistake it for reality. Today's immigrants come across the Pacific from Asia or north from Latin America, from cultures that value the family more than the individual. Immigration legislation in recent years has meant that immigrants now come with more skills, more education, and more money.

The Decline of the European Majority

Scientists who study earthquakes tell us that the North American continental plate is drifting further away from Europe. We are also moving further from Europe in our ethnic and racial composition. The descendants of European immigrants are still the majority of the population, but that majority shrank as the number of Asian Americans more than doubled between 1980 and 1990. Changes in the census definition of "other" races have reduced the comparability

Minority Growth

The North American continental plate is drifting further away from Europe. We are also moving further from Europe in our ethnic and racial composition.

(percent change in U.S. population by race and ethnicity, 1980–90)

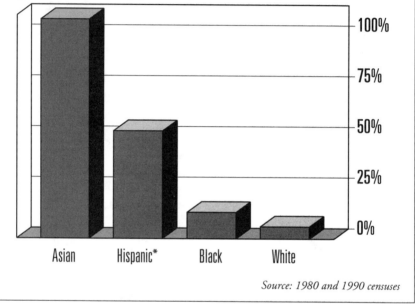

| Asian | Hispanic* | Black | White |

Source: 1980 and 1990 censuses

*Hispanics may be of any race.

of 1980 and 1990 statistics with respect to the Asian population of the United States. Bearing this in mind, the number of Asian Americans increased by 108 percent. During the same period, the Hispanic population grew 53 percent, the black population grew 13 percent, and the non-Hispanic white population grew only 4 percent.

In Canada, too, immigration has shifted from European to Asian sources. In the late 1950s and early 1960s, 90 percent of Canadian immigrants came from Europe. Seventeen of the top-20 source countries were European. By contrast, throughout the 1980s, 6 of the top 7 countries of origin were Asian. Asians accounted for almost half of all immigrants (46 percent during the decade).

Minorities are gaining larger shares of the population. Non-

Hispanic whites are steadily declining, falling from 86 percent to 84 percent of the population between 1980 and 1990. Demographer Leon Bouvier projects that less than half of the U.S. population will be non-Hispanic whites by the year 2060, and the current minority will become a majority. This is already true in 6 percent of U.S. counties, including one in Houston and two boroughs of New York City. It is on the verge of happening in other metropolitan centers like St. Louis and Fresno. On the west coast of Canada, the share of the population "of European descent" dropped 10 percent in ten years, to an estimated 78 percent in 1991.

In Canada and the U.S. alike, immigrants account for a growing proportion of population increase. Immigration itself is only part of the reason. Fertility rates among immigrants are also important. Foreign-born women in the U.S. have fertility rates 20 to 30 percent higher than those for American-born women. And whether foreign-born or not, a growing percentage of children in America are members of minorities (i.e., blacks, Hispanics, Asians, and other groups). They represented 34 percent of American children in 1990 and are projected to represent 38 percent by 2010. In California, married couples with children represent 45 percent of Hispanic households and 39 percent of Asian households but only 24 percent of non-Hispanic white households.

Minorities, Economics, and Culture

Asian Americans are a highly educated group. More than one in three (35 percent) Asian Americans aged 25 or older have completed four or more years of college, compared with only about one in five (22 percent) for all adults. They also have a high level of business ownership.

Asian-American household incomes are also higher than average. In 1988, the median income for Asian-American households was $36,449, compared with $31,569 for non-Hispanic whites, $22,691 for Hispanics, and $18,807 for blacks. Thirty-six percent of all Asian-American households had incomes of $50,000 or more, while only 28 percent of non-Hispanic whites lived in such affluent circumstances.

Only about 15 percent of Hispanic households are affluent, although the number of affluent Hispanic households nearly tripled between 1972 and 1991, from 320,000 to 959,000. Hispanics' *personal* incomes are actually lower than those of non-Hispanic whites. In both Hispanic and Asian households, however, the large number of income earners increases the *household* total. Seventy-eight percent of affluent Hispanic households have three or more people, compared with only 61 percent of affluent non-Hispanic white households. Taking all income levels into account, both Hispanic and Asian-American households had an average of about one person more (3.5 and 3.3 people, respectively) than non-Hispanic white households (2.5 people) in 1991. Instead of dispersing their earning power across multiple households, they are likely to share and share alike. Marketing to these households means taking into account their greater propensity for pulling together as a family.

United States Bank of San Francisco took account of this cultural trait among their largely Chinese customer base. It designed a "family banking" program that offered incentives like free checking when everyone in the family had an account at the bank and the combined balance exceeded $10,000. The year the family banking program was launched, deposits grew by 22 percent. Profits followed close behind.

Latin and Asian cultures are less individualistic than traditional North American and Western European cultures. Instead, they take what social scientists call a "collectivist" view of life. This has nothing to do with capitalist or communist economic systems. According to the Dutch psychologist G. Hofstede, Australia, Canada, and the U.S. have both highly individualistic cultures and capitalist economies. But some collectivist countries do not have capitalist economies. Hofstede found the best examples of these in Asian and Hispanic cultures such as Hong Kong, Taiwan, Chile, Peru, and Venezuela.

Psychologist Harry Triandis finds that in collectivist cultures, children are expected to live with their parents until they get married, and aging parents are expected to live at home with their children. Such cultures encompass about 70 percent of the world's population.

The Melting Pot Becomes a Salad Bowl

It would be easy to dismiss the collectivist strains in Hispanic and Asian-American households as a first-generation quaintness that will melt away as second- and third-generation children assimilate into mainstream American culture. This has been the trend in the past and will continue to be a factor, but there are reasons to believe that mainstream American culture exerts less homogenizing pressure on ethnic communities than it did in the past. A new term describes the way new immigrants are adapting to their new country—acculturation. Instead of giving up their language, culture, and values, they are merging them with the mainstream to alter the very fabric of American society.

The influence of the mighty American military machine on American culture has been like a noisy refrigerator motor: you never notice it until it shuts off. In fact, cuts in military budgets, especially in payroll, have removed a very powerful homogenizing force from the lives of Americans. Military service deals in conformity and uniformity. Now that fewer people are subjected to it, the natural regional and ethnic diversity of the U.S. can grow without disruption.

> ▶ **Acculturate, Not Assimilate**
>
> Hispanic and Asian immigrants of today may not assimilate into the mainstream culture as European immigrants of the past did. Instead, they are acculturating.

The homogenizing influence of military culture extends beyond the armed forces to affect people in the entire defense industry. It blankets whole regions of the country where military bases and defense plants concentrate. With the end of the Cold War, the scorching flame beneath the melting pot has been turned down to a simmer.

The postmodern family might be moribund, but the postmodern ideals of celebrating diversity are alive and well in education and the arts. The Pulitzer Prize-winning playwright Edward Albee gave a 1992 speech at Butler University in Indianapolis, in which he warned against softening the commitment to postmodernism. He said, "Any society which fears diversity and complexity, which is afraid to look at itself through anything but a funhouse mirror is in deep trouble." The celebration of diversity has gained the full blessing of the educational and artistic establishment.

▶ Celebrating Diversity

Across North America, millions of dollars are dedicated to the enhancement and preservation of ethnic, linguistic, and cultural diversity. For Asians and Hispanics, celebrating diversity means less pressure to adopt individualistic ways and more support for their traditional family orientation.

Recognizing the existence and undesirability of prejudice and racism, many government agencies and programs have adopted hiring and contracting policies that give preference to minority workers or their employers. Prejudice and racism face a countervailing force that did not exist 70 years ago when the melting pot was on full boil.

Those who do not speak English are also getting more recognition. In California, the government routinely provides many services in both English and Spanish. The Canadian federal government provides all services in English and French. The province of Quebec even has some control over its own immigration policy, so French-Canadians can better preserve their culture. A Canadian federal department exists to promote multiculturalism, and aboriginal natives in Canada are winning legal jurisdiction over large tracts of land to govern as they see fit.

Across North America, millions of dollars are dedicated to the enhancement and preservation of ethnic, linguistic, and cultural diversity. For Asians and Hispanics, celebrating diversity means less pressure to adopt individualistic ways and more support for their traditional family orientation.

Not so long ago, most products had a single national origin. Companies operated from a single country and acted on behalf of the interests of shareholders who lived there. Part of what used to make ethnic minorities eager to assimilate was hostility toward foreign competitors. Economic nationalism fueled a great deal of "us" versus "them" thinking, which spilled over into prejudice in interpersonal relations. To make certain "them" became "us," second- and third-generation immigrants adopted the ways of the dominant culture as quickly as possible.

Today, the notion of a national economy is losing its importance. Products contain parts from all over the globe, and multinational companies serve shareholders worldwide. As economic globalization increases, the international trade imperative becomes stronger, and xenophobia becomes pocketbook suicide. Again, Asians and Hispanics face less pressure to reject the strong family orientation of their cultures.

All these factors retard the rate at which second-, third-, and fourth-generation ethnics abandon their collectivist household styles. Marketing strategies that depend on increasingly individualized appeals will not work as well with Asian-American and Hispanic households. Tailoring family marketing to a particular ethnic group makes good sense given the strong family orientation of the largest and fastest-growing ethnic communities.

Ethnic Marketing

More American companies realize the value of ethnic markets and are attempting to penetrate them. Coca-Cola has succeeded impressively in the U.S., with a sweepstakes on Hispanic television. The ads and promotions feature Andrés García, the popular star of the show "El Magnate." Prizes include a Ferrari and 18 trips to Miami, each including $1,000 cash.

For many companies, ethnic marketing has focused only on correct translations and avoiding negative connotations. It is a good starting point. The tale of Pepsi's foray into the Chinese market has become a classic example of careless translation. "Come alive with the Pepsi generation!" translated as "Pepsi brings your ancestors back from the dead!"—a truly haunting slogan.

To avoid such gaffes, any translation into a non-English language should be converted back into English, by a different translator. The Pace Company of San Antonio, Texas, double-translated the label on their salsa into Spanish for the Mexican market. The translation of "no preservatives" came back into English as "without condoms." Using back-translation, they avoided a spectacular blunder.

Even within a single language, idiomatic expressions differ, and marketers should use two translators from different linguistic subgroups within the language. For example, to say that a TV show or a book "was a bomb" in England means that it caused a great sensation. In North America, the same phrase has exactly the opposite meaning. Most non-English languages have similar types of linguistic subgroup differences.

When the message is spoken, as is the case with TV or radio ads, the question of accents arises. Accents convey information about geographic origin, ethnicity, race, and social class. Radio ads for grocery items in Manila, for example, use the working-class accent because even in middle-class households the daily grocery buying is done by servants from working-class backgrounds.

POINTER #1:

▶ Avoid Language Gaffes

If you are careless about translations, you may find yourself selling resurrectionist soda or noncontraceptive condiments.

First-generation immigrants to North America prefer to deal with people of their own culture or nationality. Even when language is not a barrier, members of visibly ethnic or nonwhite groups often prefer the comfort and security of doing business with someone like themselves. One second-generation Chinese woman told me how her father always waits for the only Chinese teller at his bank to become available, even though he then proceeds to speak English throughout the transaction! Another Chinese woman told me how she chooses a bank. Her final check before opening an account is to look through the front window. If she sees no Chinese faces behind the counter, she goes to the next bank on her list.

The marketing implications are obvious. The customer-service work force must mirror the demographics of the target customer group. Companies whose most frequent contact with end consumers is via telephone have special problems. Establishing clear communication over the telephone is challenging enough when both parties speak the same language. When one party is struggling with English as well, the stage is set for frustration and dissatisfaction. Companies committed to serving particular language groups make certain that they always have bilingual staff available to handle such calls. AT&T provides interpretation services in 140 languages. The service is especially popular with emergency-service departments.

Ethnic Family Marketing

Family marketing makes marketing to ethnic communities more proactive. The marketer assimilates the values of the culture and speaks from those values. Hiring advertising, research, and marketing consultants from the target ethnic community is a quick way to become familiar with the cultural nuances that will have the greatest practical impact on your marketing.

In communities where oral tradition is still strong, illiteracy is high, and many people do not speak English, word-of-mouth advertising is king. Word-of-mouth advertising delivered through family networks can be even stronger if it is associated with family loyalty, honor, and duty. Recommendations from a senior member of a family can bring in business from the whole family. Don't treat customers just as individuals, but as ambassadors of their families.

In any type of word-of-mouth marketing, the customers must have positive things to say, and they must say them. One of the best

> ## POINTER #2:
> ▶ **Reflect the Target**
>
> Even when language is not a barrier, members of visibly ethnic or nonwhite groups often prefer the comfort and security of doing business with someone like themselves. The customer-service work force must mirror the demographics of the target customer group.

POINTER #3:

▶ Go to the People

Word-of-mouth advertising delivered through family networks can be even stronger if it is associated with family loyalty, honor, and duty. Don't treat customers just as individuals but as ambassadors of their families.

ways to encourage an ethnic community to talk about your product or service is to go where the talking gets done. In many ethnic communities, including those from Europe, the marketplace is a meeting place. People socialize as they shop. Many of their conversations center on two topics, family and shopping. The shopping discussion can start with the price of rice and end up on the interest rate on CDs. People seek and volunteer advice on everything from cantaloupes to cars.

A good strategy is to set up an outlet or point-of-sale advertisement in the ethnic language in the food-market district. You may be able to develop a partnership or agency agreement with a popular ethnic business. If the community has its own special holidays or celebrations, you may be able to win further recognition by sponsoring an event.

For many ethnic communities, the food market is the focal point for exchanging general information. Those who speak English advise those who do not. Long-time residents or those with more education advise newcomers or less-educated community members. At home or at family gatherings, those who have acquired product or market information share it with others. One woman told me how she shopped for CDs for her Italian-speaking father. She visited bank branches herself noting interest rates and the presence of any Italian-speaking staff. Since all banks had about the same rate, the discussion turned to which bank would treat him with the most respect. She recommended a bank with an Italian-speaking staff member, and that is where he went.

In many parts of the world, the word of a community member is worth more than the word of an outside entity like a company. To earn trust, a company's advertising might feature employees who also live in the community. The employees should have titles of respect, and their faces should be displayed to demonstrate that your company employs people who will put their personal reputation on the line. This inspires trust.

Honor is another key to family-oriented ethnic markets. Members of many cultures are accustomed to the respect they get from their family name. They are also socialized never to betray their family's good name. In some cultures, even the suggestion that one would betray one's family is an insult. For this reason, members of some ethnic groups may interpret normal business legalities as a sign of mistrust or even disrespect toward their family name.

Businesses can do several things to avoid misunderstandings. At the very least, staff can apologize for the necessity of paperwork. Companies can also institute special policies to ease credit approvals, on the authority of a local manager who specializes in serving that community.

> ▶ The Future Is Ethnic

As ethnic groups become more American and America becomes more ethnic, those who hone their family marketing skills in ethnic markets today will find themselves well prepared for the mass markets of tomorrow.

Employees from the community with the authority to negotiate freely can also prevent the loss of business due to differences in business etiquette. For example, North Americans can easily be offended by a buyer's last-minute attempts to renegotiate a price after goods have been delivered or by a buyer's expectations of a "gift" from a vendor to show appreciation for the buyer's patronage. In some countries, however, these tactics are standard practice.

Some families are ethnic community leaders. Those with more education or wealth have more influence than similarly endowed individuals in mainstream society. A recommendation from a senior member of a prominent family is invaluable. Business development specialists for any ethnic market should be especially proactive in developing relations with such leading families. They should also have the authority to deal with these people according to their own business customs.

Asian and Hispanic consumers continue to be the fastest-growing ethnic groups in America. Their collectivist family orientations will not disappear quickly across successive generations. In the past, only marketers who targeted these groups had to understand their greater family focus. In the not-too-distant future, the family orientations of Asians and Hispanics will become America's orientation. Those who hone their family marketing skills in ethnic markets today will find themselves well prepared for the mass markets of tomorrow.

REFERENCES

American Diversity. American Demographics Desk Reference Series, No. 1, July 1991, p. 20.

Associated Press. "Writers in Artistic Sleep, Albee Warns." *The Vancouver Sun,* September 30, 1992, p. C5.

Center for the Continuing Study of the California Economy. *California Population Characteristics 1990.* Palo Alto, CA: 1990.

Exter, Thomas. "Middle-Aging Asians," *American Demographics,* November 1992, p. 67.

Fost, Dan. "San Antonio Salsa Succeeds in Sonora." *American Demographics,* September 1992, p. 10.

Fouke, Carol. "Asian-American Market More Important than Ever." *Marketing News,* October 14, 1991, p. 19.

Goerne, Carrie. "Targeting Hispanics: NutraSweet Educates While Coke Titillates." *Marketing News,* November 11, 1991, pp. 1-2.

Hofstede, G. "Dimensions of National Cultures in Fifty Countries and Three Regions." *Expiscations in Cross-Cultural Psychology.* Deregowski, J.B., Dziurawiec, S., and Annis, R.C., editors. Lisse, The Netherlands: Swets & Zeitinger B.V., 1983, pp. 335-355.

REFERENCES

Hofstede, G. *Culture's Consequences.* Beverly Hills, CA: Sage, 1980.

Hogben, David. "AT&T Offers Interpreting Service to Bridge Language Gap." *The Vancouver Sun,* September 18, 1992, p. D9.

Ignacio, Monique. Personal communication, Charlie Agatep Associates, Quezon City, Phillippines, 1991.

Logan, Ronald. "Immigration During the 1980s." *Canadian Social Trends,* Vol. 20, Spring 1991, pp. 10-13.

McRae, Donald. cited in "Boomers Won't Find Plain Vanilla Future." *The Vancouver Sun,* October 6, 1990, p. A6.

National Center for Health Statisitics. *Monthly Vital Statistics Report, 38,* 12, 1989.

Newcomb, Theodore M. *Personality and Social Change.* New York: Dryden, 1943.

O'Hare, William. "A New Look at Asian Americans." *American Demographics,* October 1990, pp. 26-31.

O'Hare, William. "The Rise of Hispanic Affluence." *American Demographics,* August 1990, p. 40-43.

Russell, Cheryl. "Throw Out the Script." *American Demographics,* September 1990, p. 2.

Statistics Canada. *Current Demographic Analysis— Report on the Demographic Situtation in Canada 1988.* Catalogue 91-209E, 1989.

Triandis, Harry C., *et al.* "Individualism and Collectivism: Cross-Cultural Perspectives on Self-Ingroup Relationships." *Journal of Personality and Social Psychology,* 54, 1988, pp. 323-338.

U.S. Bureau of the Census, 1991 Current Population Survey, Washington, D.C.

U.S. Bureau of the Census, 1992 Current Population Survey, Washington, D.C.

Waldrop, Judith and Thomas Exter. "What the 1990 Census Will Show." *American Demographics*, January 1990, p. 25.

▼▼▼▼▼▼▼

PART II

How to Do
Family
Marketing

▲▲▲▲▲▲▲

CHAPTER SIX

Principles of Family Marketing

When we view the family as a consuming unit, we market *to* it. When we look at the family as a social environment for individuals, we market *through* families. No hard-and-fast rule distinguishes marketing to families from marketing through families, but a good marketing plan will likely contain elements of both.

In general, marketing *to* families assumes that members do joint decisionmaking and consumption, especially those who live together. Marketing *through* families is more likely to involve relatives outside the immediate family household. Marketing through family members often means influencing them to recommend your product or service to one another.

Family as Unit vs. Family as Social Environment

The core strategy of family marketing is to influence purchase decisions by speaking *to*, and *through*, family relationships. The tactics of achieving this influence are familiar to most marketers. Family marketing is different because consumers' relationships with one another are brought into the analysis of their relationships with the product.

Sociologists, social psychologists, and consumer psychologists have developed various models of family decisionmaking. Their efforts, while methodologically and statistically elegant, usually cover only a narrow range of family configurations. The literature is biased toward defining families as households containing husbands and wives. Much of the scholarly research done during the 1980s focused on the effects of shifting gender roles, married women's career orientations, and the balance of influence and power between spouses.

▶ **Narrowing the Focus**

Social scientists have developed various models of family decisionmaking, but their studies tend to define families as households containing husbands and wives. Marketers, by contrast, do not confine themselves to any particular household configuration. If the best market turns out to be single-parent households or traditional gender-role households, then and only then do practical marketers narrow their focus.

Marketing practitioners, by contrast, do not confine themselves *a priori* to any particular household configuration. If their best market turns out to be single-parent households or traditional gender-role households, then and only then do practical marketers narrow their focus. This chapter outlines a model of family decisionmaking that addresses the needs of most marketing practitioners. In general, it applies to all types of families and households and uses simple but robust concepts and variables that cover most of the factors involved in purchase decisions.

The model of family decisionmaking presented here builds on familiar concepts used in marketing to individuals. Individual-oriented marketing tries to influence purchase decisions by influencing individuals. The tactics promote an exchange relationship between the vendor and the purchaser.

Family marketing ideally does everything that individual marketing does, and more. In addition to promoting an exchange relationship with the purchase decision maker, family marketing seeks to address the complicated relationships between purchasers and consumers within the multiperson context of families.

A Model for Family Decisionmaking

The following is an example of the complexity inherent in family decisionmaking. In a nuclear family with two parents and two children, the older child initiates a product search by asking for a bicycle as a birthday present. In this case, the consumer initiates the purchase, but only decides the product category, not the brand.

The parents then discuss the idea to confirm a price range. The mother in this case is a nonconsuming purchase decision maker whose main input is to veto or approve particular price ranges. The younger child may constrain the duration and location of the shopping by insisting that a trip to his or her favorite fast-food outlet be included in the outing. Retailers distant from the restaurant then fall off the shopping list. The younger sibling, therefore, is a nonconsumer who unconsciously influences the buying process. The father seeks further input from the birthday child about cosmetic features such as color, but goes on to impose additional criteria of his own, like durability and safety, when choosing the final brand and model.

The complexity of this scenario illustrates why it is useful to have a family decisionmaking model. A family marketing program must systematically consider the most typical purchase scenarios, the distribution of the consumer and decision maker functions across family members, and the distribution of those functions throughout different scenarios.

It can be profitable to take the complexity of family decisionmaking into account when developing a marketing plan. The cost of doing so, however, must not exceed the anticipated additional profit. One must have quick and easy ways to reduce complexity to essentials that affect marketing strategy. The remainder of this chapter presents a model to help marketers quickly zero in on the essentials of family decisionmaking for their product or service. It helps to answer the key questions on the next page.

1. Who's buying for whom?

Which family members will consume the product and which will participate in the purchase decision? How much overlap is there between the consumers and the decision makers?

2. Who are the principal characters?

Who are current and desired consumers and purchase decision makers (PDMs)? What are their demographic profiles? What kind of family structures do they live in? Are any relatives or outsiders involved in the purchase?

3. What's the plot for the purchase?

What are the steps in a typical purchase? What initiates it? Do different people have different roles in the sequence? Who performs which functions? Is each step repeated with each purchase, or is there an abbreviated sequence for subsequent purchases? Is there a special scenario for changing brands?

4. Who wants what when?

What benefits do each of the players seek at each stage of the process? In addition to product-related costs and benefits, what do various influencers want from the purchase process?

5. What can we assume?

What do we know about family decisionmaking? How can consumer psychology and marketing simplify the planning process?

This model points out the principal factors that marketers should take into account in most cases. But each target market is different, and the questions above may not cover all possibilities. Likewise, not all of the questions are relevant to every product. The model applies to one product or service at a time. Any family can, and probably does, use variations of the model for different products. For example, ordering a home-delivered pizza is usually a joint decision, while the person who buys vacuum-cleaner bags might never discuss it at all with other family members.

Purchasers and Consumers

In individual marketing, an individual plays both decision maker and consumer roles. A family marketing approach extends the range of possible purchaser/consumer relationships in three areas. There can be more than one decision maker and more than one consumer, and they may be different people. A single framework or model can integrate these three areas, as shown in the table on the next page.

Each of the 18 cells in the model represents a different pattern of purchaser/consumer relationship. The purchase decision makers can be a single individual, a subset of individuals in the family, or all the members of the family. Likewise, the consumers can be one, some, or all family members. In addition, the product may be purchased for oneself or for someone else. Some decision makers may consume the product, while others may not.

Separating the product-consumer role from the purchase decision maker role is a fundamental difference between family marketing and individual marketing. This means that consumer preferences may

> ▶ **Extending Customer Relationships**
>
> A family marketing approach extends the range of possible purchaser/consumer relationships in three areas. There can be more than one decision maker and more than one consumer, and they may be different people.

Who Decides vs. Who Consumes

A family purchase decision falls into 1 of 18 categories, depending on the answer to this question: "Is anyone making the purchase decision also using the product or service purchased?"

PURCHASE DECISION MAKERS

		ONE MEMBER		SOME MEMBERS		ALL MEMBERS	
CONSUMERS	ONE MEMBER	yes	no	yes	no	yes	no*
	SOME MEMBERS	yes	no	yes	no	yes	no*
	ALL MEMBERS	yes	no*	yes	no*	yes	no*

* These roles presume a transfer of goods between separate family households, as in gift-giving among relatives.

not be directly expressed in marketplace purchases. For example, children who want very sweet breakfast cereal might not get it if mom decides they shouldn't have it. Then again, they may be able to influence her, especially if they accompany her to the food store. In either case, the consumer's preference affects the purchase decision indirectly, through the purchase decisionmaking of another family member who does not consume the product.

Special dynamics arise when consumers and decision makers overlap. The issue gets more complicated when decision makers don't have an equal interest in the outcome. Those who play dual roles (i.e., both purchaser and consumer) have an edge over those who play only a single role. When a group of decision makers includes both consumers and nonconsumers, consumers have a certain amount of expert influence. Since they know what the consumer wants, objections to their preferences must be based on other grounds.

A group of consumers may disagree among themselves about which marketplace option they would jointly choose. Ultimately, however, their choices can only be translated into purchases by a decision maker. Therefore, the consumer who is a sole decision maker has an automatic veto. Likewise, a consumer who is one of several decision makers while other consumers are not, can raise the specter of a decision-maker veto to constrain the set of choices considered by the consumer group. In more complex situations, other consumers may be able to make it costly for a decision maker to exercise a veto.

In any case, it is clear that one must understand the distribution of consumer and decision maker roles within a family before developing a family marketing plan. The model aggregates purchasers and consumers into three broad categories based on the number of people sharing a role: one, some, and all.

The single purchase decision maker stands as a conduit to the marketplace for the consumers' preferences. He or she can also use personal discretion to modify the signal sent to the marketplace.

The single decision maker bears some resemblance to an agent or broker in industrial marketing. For example, some insurance brokers act as agents for several insurance companies. They simultaneously act as PDMs (purchase decision makers) for their clients. A broker could have a client bent on buying one particular term of insurance for no good reason. If the broker had the client's best interests at heart and discovered a company offering longer-term coverage for the same price, the broker might alter the client's demands when he actually books a policy in the insurance marketplace.

This analogy is limited because the relationships between family members are usually much closer than those between brokers and clients. The choices of consuming family members impact directly and forcefully on the decision maker in the family. For example, the mother who buys her child sugar-saturated cereal may have to deal with a hyperactive child after breakfast. This makes the decision maker in a family more likely to moderate or alter consumer preferences than is the case in an arms-length business relationship.

It is important to examine the amount of input the single decision maker accepts from other family members regarding the purchase. If the decision maker takes no input, the marketing problem devolves into the familiar individual marketing case. In individual marketing, the marketer focuses on the principal purchaser. If one can safely assume that other family members have little or no input into the purchase decision, family marketing is the same as marketing to an individual. However, there are relatively few products or services that other family members have nothing to say about. For example, other family members may not know as much as mom does about which clothing stores offer the best values, but they do have plenty to say about what they want to wear.

When a single decision maker takes the preferences of other family members into account, we are marketing *through* the family. The marketing strategy is to activate consumers to express their preferences for your product to the decision maker.

▶ Accepting Input

Few products or services can escape the complexity of family-level decisionmaking, even if one person is making the actual purchase. When a single decision maker takes the preferences of other family members into account, we are marketing through the family.

When several family members are decision makers, it is more difficult for one of them to modify consumer preferences. In addition, it is also more likely that at least one of the decision makers is also a consumer.

Different psychological forces act when some but not all family members are decision makers. Some may not be interested, while others may have no time to spend or knowledge about the product category. The possibilities are so numerous that these cases always require more information. The best place to start is to look at who the decision makers are and aren't and determine whether they share common demographic (e.g., gender and age) or psychological (e.g., technical knowledge and interest) characteristics. The same is true when only some family members are consumers. For example, tricycles are consumed by the family members with only very young demographic profiles.

The decision maker has the most difficult task when everyone in the family is a consumer. He or she must acknowledge, if not satisfy, the diverse preferences of all family members.

A product that offers interpersonal harmony is helpful when divergent preferences and tastes could become embarrassing or threatening. Blue Nun played this angle as the wine that goes with anything. At restaurants, families usually order only a single wine at a time, which forces some family members to modify their menu choices to fit one wine type. Blue Nun leapt into the breach by offering a middle-of-the-road wine that would go with any menu choice. It also offered anyone playing "wine connoisseur" a convenient way to avoid displaying ignorance.

At special times of the year like Christmas and Thanksgiving, or when products have a high social component in their joint consumption (e.g., pizzas, holiday travel, amusements), the decision maker group is more likely to include the entire family. In a 1980 article in the *Journal of Consumer Research*, Pierre Filiatrault and Brent Ritchie suggest that joint decisionmaking is more likely when:

> ▶ **Compromise**
>
> When everyone in the family is a consumer, the decision maker must acknowledge if not satisfy the diverse preferences of all family members.

- the perceived risk associated with the decision is high
- ample time is available for the decision
- the family places greater importance on the decision
- there are no children in the family
- the family is middle income
- the family is a younger family
- the family contains two spouses but only one breadwinner

When all members of the family are also decision makers, a special dynamic emerges. When the family acts as "a family," family myths and history are more likely to influence the process. At the same time, the need to find compromise products or decision strategies (e.g., coin tossing, turn taking) is greatest.

Family Purchasing Agent

The family purchasing-agent pattern is a traditional one, where one person, usually a full-time homemaker, makes most of the purchase decisions for the household, especially for small frequent purchases of nondurables like food and housewares. The breadwinner might make decisions about large-ticket items like cars. The children get no say in decisions for jointly consumed items. This pattern can co-exist comfortably with individual decisions and purchases. For example, children might make their own decisions about what beverages to buy at the school cafeteria. Mom, however, may have decided what clothes they are wearing to school.

> ▶ **Purchase Patterns**
>
> The purchasing-agent pattern, gift-giving pattern, and father-and-son pattern might all apply to the same family in different situations.

Gift Giving

The "joint decisionmaking for a third-party consumer" pattern typifies what happens in gift-giving. In this pattern, the gift-givers talk over what would be an appropriate gift for the recipient. This pattern can also apply, however, when the recipient totally depends on the decision makers.

This pattern also applies to products consumed by a subset of family members who are not the decision makers. In such cases, the influence of the consumers on the decision makers is more complex. The decision makers must take into account the relationship between the consumers. For example, when a mother is buying sodas for her children, her husband might suggest that getting one large bottle would cause less squabbling between the kids than two smaller bottles of different flavors.

Family Roles

This pattern shows the women in the family cooperating to both make the purchase decision and consume the product. Products like tampons or nail-polish remover might be bought in this pattern. The same could be said of razor blades and shaving cream for fathers and sons.

The abstract roles of consumer and purchaser in the model can be replaced by common family-relation roles like dad, mom, son, and daughter. The model applies to all types of families regardless of the specific familial relationships, which could just as easily be that of step-father, great-aunt, adopted son, or daughter-in-law.

REFERENCES

Filiatrault, Pierre and J.R. Brent Ritchie. "Joint Purchasing Decisions: A Comparison of Influence Structure in Family and Couple Decisionmaking." *Journal of Consumer Research, 7,* September 1980, pp. 131-140.

Qualls, William J. "Household Decision Behavior: The Impact of Husbands' and Wives' Sex Role Orientation." *Journal of Consumer Research, 14,* September 1987, pp. 264-279.

CHAPTER SEVEN

The Drama of Family Marketing

Good marketing starts with good marketing research. Good research starts with asking the right questions. If your product is in an established category, you need to know who buys your product and who buys competitors' products. If your aim is to increase business from existing customers, you must know how your primary customers' families differ from your secondary customers' families.

The trick is to decide which questions will best help narrow down your profile of customers' families. Good prospects are factors that might distinguish family members who make purchase decisions about your product from those who do not. For example, the product itself might be designed for a specific demographic segment (e.g., razor blades for males older than age 14 or so).

Principal Characters

Compare any previous research findings with the standard family profile of your trading area. What kinds of families are over- or under-represented among your customers or potential customers? For example, a sports-equipment manufacturer might notice that female-headed single-parent families are under-represented among

▶Consumer Roles

THE INITIATOR instigates a purchase, but may or may not be the actual consumer.

THE INFLUENCER may recommend, reject, or otherwise affect a purchase, but has nothing else to do with it.

THE PURCHASER may be either decision maker or consumer, or both, or neither.

households that buy fishing gear. If so, the manufacturer might want to know if father-son combinations are over-represented in customer households. What are the most common ages of sons in these households?

Once you have descriptions of the demographic and family structure of customers and potential customers, you can focus further research on members of these families. You can start answering questions about their motivations, media habits, and decisionmaking processes for your product category. Chapter Eight examines research techniques that are most appropriate for answering such questions about families.

Going beyond the demographic profiles of families, you must also discover more about the specific tasks involved in the family decisionmaking process. This process must be tailored to specific products and to specific family structures. The roles of purchase decision maker and consumer are certainly not the only functional roles involved in the process leading up to a purchase, but they are the two that most sharply distinguish family marketing from marketing to individuals. In his 1985 book *The Dynamics of Consumer Behavior*, consumer psychologist Winston Mahatoo describes some of the other roles.

The *initiator* is often the consumer, but not always. For example, parents whose adult daughter has invited them to her wedding may purchase airline tickets. The parents "consume" and pay for the flight, but the daughter initiated the purchase.

In families where the decision makers do not speak English, the English-speaking members may be enlisted to *gather informa-*

tion about the options available in the marketplace. For example, a young daughter might phone around for information on building supplies for a non-English-speaking father who is planning a home renovation.

Even though all roles involve influence, sometimes an individual or group *influences* a purchase decision without playing any other role. For example, at a family gathering, a brother-in-law might tell another how happy he was with a particular brand of gas barbecue grill. Before buying a personal computer, a young woman might phone her brother for advice on which features to seek.

It is also important to remember that influence can be exerted toward or away from a product or brand. For example, an independence-seeking teenager might steer clear of soft drinks that his parents prefer. Mom and dad in this case exert a negative influence on the purchase decision.

The *purchaser* may not be a decision maker or consumer. For example, a man who picks up feminine-hygiene products for his wife and is told exactly what to get is neither the decision maker nor the consumer. Usually, however, the purchaser must make some last-minute decisions. In the above example, a man might have two stores to choose from. When he gets into the store, he might notice a sale on a larger box, even though it was not the size his wife specified. Then he must decide what he thinks she would choose, given this new information. There are so many small decisions in making even the most mundane purchase that purchasers are rarely entirely left out of the decisionmaking process.

Specific roles come into play for each product. Buying and chewing bubble gum might not involve as many roles as buying and driving a car. Robert Ferber and Lucy Lee, professors of business administration, studied the role of *family financial officer* (FFO). The FFO was defined as the person who "looks after payment of the bills, keeps track of expenditures, and decides on the use of leftover funds at the end of the pay period." Ferber and Lee found that the probability of different product purchases depended on whether the FFO was the husband or the wife. When the husband was the FFO, the family had more savings, had assets in a greater variety of investments, and bought cars less frequently.

About half of the newlyweds Ferber and Lee studied played the role jointly. One year after marriage, only 37 percent were still doing so. If the wife was more economy- or value- or bargain-minded than the husband, she was more likely to take on this role. The use of more conservative savings products was associated with both spouses continuing to play the FFO role jointly.

> ## ▶ Role-Playing
>
> To plan a family marketing approach, merge demographic and family information with what you know about the roles people play.

With all of the above functional roles, you need to know which family members, if any, typically play which role for decisions about your product or service category. Is the initiator usually a child under age 10? Is the purchaser as likely to be a husband as a wife? Planning a family marketing approach involves merging demographic and family structure information with knowledge about the functional roles people play out in making purchase decisions.

Even within a single product category, families periodically abandon one decisionmaking pattern and replace it with another. If a teenager gets a driver's license, the family's decision about where to buy car insurance could change from a single-person decision to a two- or three-person decision.

The Plot

For a family to buy your product or service, you need to know more about how they make decisions in that product category. The common roles that are played in the decisionmaking process are only part of what you must know. You also need to know if there are any regular steps, stages, or phases in the decisionmaking. Are the roles arranged in a sequence that accomplishes some of the steps before others? In other words, what script does the family typically follow to make a decision?

Using a metaphor from drama, we can talk about the phases of the decisionmaking process as "acts" in a play. Each act contains smaller segments, or "scenes."

In a June 1974 article in the *Journal of Consumer Research*, Harry Davis and Benny Rigaux looked at husband-and-wife decisionmaking for 25 different products. They divided the decisionmaking process into three sequential acts: problem recognition, information search, and the final decision. In the first act, problem recognition, husbands and wives tended to have more equal influence. During the second act, information search, one or the other spouse tended to dominate. The household division of labor tended to affect which spouse would seek information for which products. Wives tended to seek information on children's clothing, while husbands tended to seek information on insurance purchases. In the third and concluding act, the decision, husband and wife came together again with more equal influence.

▶ **Three Acts**

I: Recognizing the problem or need

II: Searching for information

III: Making the purchase decision

For many products (e.g., family vacations, living-room furniture), husbands and wives tended to share in decisionmaking throughout. For a few of the 25 products, all decisions were made by one spouse, and it was as likely to be the husband as the wife (e.g., garden tools, alcoholic beverages).

Planning a family marketing approach requires recognizing the principal characters in each of these acts. During the first "act," problem recognition, your marketing tasks revolve around the motivations of the main character and the benefits he or she might want. In the information search phase, the second act, the chief marketing tasks concern communicating with the lead player. If the lead in the first act is different from the lead in the second act, you must also deal with how to influence their communications in the final act. The challenge is to ensure that every player in the family makes a decision that favors your product when their scene comes up.

Davis and Rigaux did not consider other potential acts in the

▶ The Performance

Families take longer to make a purchase decision the first time than the 50th, i.e., the first performance has more acts and scenes. For subsequent purchases, however, the script becomes habitual and abbreviated.

decisionmaking process. After deciding which product to buy, for example, the players may still need to decide *where* and *how* to buy the product. Consuming the product is also important, because that is when family members talk to each other about their satisfaction with the decision.

For services, purchase and consumption are one and the same. For example, when you buy a car wash, you cannot take it home and save it in the refrigerator until your car gets dirtier. If experts on services marketing are correct, the combined purchase/consumption act could well be the most important one in the entire decisionmaking process. It is full of what they call "moments of truth," when customers evaluate their satisfaction with the service.

Services marketing consultants Chip Bell and Ron Zemke urge service managers to reconceptualize their jobs as theater play directors. The employees who provide front-line services are the live actors. The customers are the audience in an audience-participation play. Managers must anticipate the many directions members of the audience might take in each scenario and empower and prepare the actors to provide satisfaction, come what may.

Like individuals, families take longer to make a purchase decision the first time than the 50th. Or in our play analogy, the first performance has more acts and scenes. For subsequent purchases, however, most of the decisions have already been made, and often the only question remaining is when to buy. The script becomes habitual and abbreviated.

This is especially significant in two common marketing situations. First, introducing a new category of product or service always involves dealing with customers who are going through the decisionmaking process for the first time. In this case, it is not possible to identify any preexisting typical script. A family marketing approach to a new category launch means working intensively with a few test families to observe and develop convenient and satisfying scripts.

Second, attempting to take market share away from a competitor means encouraging potential customers to lengthen their routine script by putting more choices back into it. Essentially, this means getting someone in the family to "open a scene" regarding the purchase.

The script metaphor is more applicable to some types of purchases than others. The amount of regularity in the script makes a difference to its usefulness as a tool for planning a marketing strategy. At one extreme, some scripts are so loose that little or no pattern in the sequence of steps can be identified. At the tight extreme, there may be only a single script, with an unvarying set of scenes.

> ## ▶ Variations on a Theme
>
> Some products have multiple scripts, some purchases have different acts, and consumers may play different scenes from one performance to the next.

Other products have clear but bewilderingly numerous scripts. There could be dozens of sets for buying a soft drink (e.g., vending machine, fast-food outlet, tavern, grocery store, hot-dog stand, etc.). Products that people can purchase through multiple scripts require much more marketing planning. In practice, this is not usually as daunting as it sounds. The players often turn out to be the same people in different scenes, and the scripts often turn out to be comparatively simple.

In a 1981 article in *American Psychologist*, Robert Abelson, a social psychologist at Yale, described the general concept of a script and the ways in which scripts can be more tightly or loosely defined. Scripts can differ from one another in other ways. For example, the acts may be ordered differently. Products bought on impulse may completely lack an information-search act, or the information search may occur after the purchase. Likewise, within acts, actors play different numbers of scenes from one performance to the next. In taking a child to a hairdresser, for example, a parent might want a shampoo and cut on one visit, but just a haircut on the next.

Motivations and Benefits

In any purchasing script, each player has a motive. All of them are seeking to solve problems or attain benefits. Individual marketing studies cover this thoroughly, and there is substantial literature on customer satisfaction and multi-attribute decisionmaking. Marketers wishing to take a family marketing approach must first make certain they have addressed the appeal of their product to individuals.

As many marketers have discovered, however, the link between the product and the benefit sought by the consumer is only part of the story. Even when individuals see a product that offers the benefits they want, they often buy a different product. They do not act to optimize their personal benefit.

Why don't people consistently act in their own self-interest? Often, the reason is that they are buying as part of a family. As a single member of a larger social unit, an individual takes into account the benefits to the group. Group benefits include consequences that arise from interpersonal interactions involved in making the buying decision. In family purchase decisions, the buying process itself has costs and benefits to family members.

Sometimes people will forego their preferred brand or store or payment method to see other family members enjoy their first choice. In such cases, interpersonal motives take precedence over personal ones. In family marketing, you must discover whether people have social motivations to select your product or service. A fast-food family restaurant might not offer the cuisine or ambiance that parents want, but they go there anyway because the children may cause a scene otherwise. Likewise, in families with traditional gender roles, homemakers seek appreciation and recognition for their cooking and cleaning. These are tasks that bring the purchase of food and cleaning products into the shared consumption scene. Homemakers choose one product over another based on the appreciation or criticism they may receive from other family members.

A family member who expresses a much stronger preference

than those expressed by other family members is likely to have greater influence. Those with weaker preferences want to avoid conflict. Deferring to the family member with the strongest preference has two interpersonal consequences: it maintains family peace, and it expresses affection toward the member with the strongest preference.

In a study of married couples, Kim Corfman and Donald Lehmann found that intensity was one of the strongest predictors of whose preference would prevail in a joint decisionmaking task where both spouses were decision makers and consumers, for two reasons. First, spouses with weaker preferences wanted their partners to be happy and to get what they needed. They took pleasure in each other's pleasure. Second, neither spouse wanted to initiate a conflict, and felt pain in each other's pain. Michael Menasco and David Curry confirmed this conclusion in a 1989 study of husband/wife decisionmaking.

> ▶ **Who Wants What?**
>
> Deferring to the family member with the strongest preference has two interpersonal consequences: it maintains family peace, and it expresses affection toward the member with the strongest preference.

To apply this to family marketing, encourage one member of the family to adamantly voice his or her preference for your product. Simultaneously, tell the other players that in accepting your product they show love and affection toward the family member who prefers the product.

Corfman and Lehmann also found that when spouses' preferences were different but equally strong, they resorted to a relationship-maintaining strategy of turn taking. Over time, each partner tended to "win" an equal number of times. Menasco and Curry elaborated on this finding by pointing out that the intensity with which each partner wanted the option they won or lost made little difference. It was instead the *number* of wins and losses that counted.

Apparently, the intensity of the preference only has an impact on the decision at hand. When the same problem comes up again, the strength of the family member's preference during the previous process is ignored. Only their preference is carried forward, and how strong it was is disregarded.

Most real-life decisions are multi-optioned, and each option has costs and benefits that appeal differently to each member of the household. Families may only resort to turn-taking when the search for compromise options has failed to produce a solution within a reasonable amount of time. The implication is that your product will be chosen more often if people view it as an honorable compromise option in a product category where several family members typically have equally strong preferences.

The FIRO (Fundamental Interpersonal Relations Orientation) group dynamics theory of William Schutz describes three general interpersonal motives that operate in most family decisions. Since these motives are so common, it is worth asking yourself to what extent they operate in the purchase scripts for your product or service.

The first motive is inclusion. The family member or members who identify the need must decide with whom to share it. This often takes place in the first or second "scene" in "act" one. The family members in the initiator role must decide if the purchase will be individual or cooperative and whether they will share the decision, or the consumption, or both.

> ▶ **Three Motives**
>
> **1. INCLUSION—** Sometimes, no one wants to be left out.
>
> **2. CONTROL—** Those who bring up issues or veto decisions have more power than figureheads.
>
> **3. AFFECTION—** Family members may sacrifice personal preferences for the sake of a loved one.
>
> *Source: William Schutz*

For some purchases, no one wants to be left out. Products that offer something for everyone help the family meet these desiderata. Many parents dismiss cruises as family holidays because there is typically so little for young children to enjoy. Carnival Cruise Lines solved the problem by offering a seven-day cruise to the Bahamas that includes a trip to Walt Disney World in Orlando, Florida.

Marketers should look carefully at who might be involved in making or breaking purchases of their products. Imagine a single-parent family that lacks after-school child care. If the eldest child joins a Little League baseball team, the entire family is affected. The family will spend several hours each week at the ballpark and will have to spend some time in sporting-goods stores. The responsibility for the decision rapidly moves from the eldest child to the family, because it now affects and includes everyone.

As a manufacturer of children's sports gear, a family marketing approach would lead you to ask how common such scenarios are. You would want to know how you could minimize the exercise of vetoes by other family members when the prospective Little Leaguer puts joining the team on the family agenda. You would ask whether the retail chains you sell through can make shopping easier for other family members. Do retail outlets in malls appeal to all ages? Do these outlets have merchandise that appeals to all ages and physical-exercise interests? If not, how could you extend your own product line to fill this gap?

> ▶ **The Agenda**
>
> The greatest power is often vested in the person who raised the issue in the first place. Market your product to those who put items on the agenda.

The second motive in Schutz's FIRO theory, normally played out during the second act, is control. Family members work out role specializations and dominance relations in various task areas. One might become the information seeker, another might check the finances, and a third might schedule the purchase or consumption.

In watching a family arrive at a group decision, it is easy to misconstrue the impact each person has. There is a tendency in observers to attribute the greatest power to the person who declares the decision made. In some senses, however, the announcement of the final decision is made by an individual in a passive powerless role, often the titular head of the family.

The greatest power is often vested in the person who raised the issue in the first place. In many families, children can put a question on the agenda for family decisionmaking as easily as adults. Market your product to those who put items on the agenda.

A person who can *veto* a decision also has enormous power in family decisionmaking. A veto, of course, can only operate with the consent of other family members. The rest of the family can always accept a price for overturning a veto. The question for marketers then is, "Whose objections will carry the most weight?"

Marketers must address the objections raised by those who can make their objections stick. Suppose a family is on a road trip and is stopping at a restaurant. One of the children is not wearing shoes, and the family can't go in the restaurant unless he puts them on. The child says, "I'm not going to wear them, and you can't make me!" Short of physically wrestling with an uncooperative, kicking child, the parents have little choice. The child has effectively vetoed the restaurant option. If this were an isolated case, it would not matter, but if research showed that former regular patrons stopped coming as soon as their oldest child reached age 3, it would matter.

The third motive in Schutz's FIRO theory is affection. In making buying decisions, family members express solidarity, enjoy each other's enjoyment, and appreciate each other's task-related work. Concerns about these interpersonal accomplishments are most likely to be felt during the third act, in the decision phase.

When the family is clear on who is in on the decision and who will do what, they can deal with interpersonal relationships. As Menasco and Curry found, family members make decisions that will benefit their loved ones. Husbands and wives want the best for each other and for their children. Affection also operates in transgenerational buying decisions. One family I studied included a great-grandmother, three grandmothers, five daughters, and a dozen grandchildren. The middle-aged young adult women cooperated every Christmas to give the great-grandmother a big box of candy from her favorite chocolate maker. The box would be given to her in the presence of all the daughters and granddaughters, and they would demolish it together in a chocolate-eating orgy. Some of the daughters did not particularly like that brand of chocolates but chose it each year because it was great-grandmother's favorite.

Factors that establish or maintain family identity can influence purchase decisions. Choosing a family vacation is a good example. Families that choose museums and science centers may be saying, "We're an intellectual family." Families that choose beaches and water parks might identify with "We're active and fun-loving," while families that take separate vacations might be saying, "We're all strong-willed and independent."

Common Family Dynamics

Newlyweds tend to make decisions together. As they gradually get to know each others' areas of expertise and task preferences, they begin to specialize. The husband takes over more of some purchase decisions, while the wife takes over others. It used to be easy to predict which decisions would be the husband's and which would be the wife's. Today, however, fewer families have a traditional gender role orientation, and husband-wife couples are also a smaller share of all families. In many product categories, more research is needed to know who will end up making the major decisions in today's new families.

For products aimed at newlyweds, the tendency toward joint decisionmaking must be taken into account. Even in blended families, there is likely an abbreviated period of task-sorting following remarriage.

James U. McNeal, professor of marketing at Texas A&M University and author of the recent book *Kids As Customers*, has studied the mutual influence children and parents have on each other's purchases. He says children's influences on family purchases have increased in recent years for several reasons. For one thing, parents have fewer children, and with less sibling competition, each child gets more input. For another thing, single parents and working couples have less time for shopping than the traditional, single-breadwinner nuclear family. They there-

> ▶ **Division of Labor**
>
> Couples start out making lots of joint decisions, then begin to specialize. It used to be easy to predict who did what, but that is less true today.

fore encourage the child to be more self-reliant and to contribute more to maintaining the household. Finally, McNeal says that women who have children later in life have more to spend on what children want. Since there are more older first-time mothers today, the children of those mothers influence the spending of a larger share of marketplace dollars.

McNeal notes that 2-to-3-year-old children make marketplace choices, even if only in terms of food flavors and clothes colors. By age 5 or 6, children have learned to manipulate their parents' purchases with finesse. McNeal estimates that children between the ages of 2 and 12 influence about $132 billion in parental purchase decisions annually.

In a study reported in the March 1989 issue of the *Journal of Consumer Research*, Ellen Foxman, Patriya Tansuhaj, and Karin Ekstrom asked parents and teenagers about the influence teens had in buying decisions for 12 items. Generally, all agreed that parents had more influence, and teens had some influence. The teenagers had the greatest influence over decisions about low-cost items for their own consumption (e.g., records, magazines, clothes, toothpaste). Teens had the least influence on high-cost items consumed by the family (e.g, living-room furniture, family car).

▶ Kid Consumers

Children influence billions of dollars of parental purchases every year. They also have more family shopping responsibility.

Because both parents work in more families today, children have greater shopping responsibilities. A national survey by Teen-age Research Unlimited, of Lake Forest, Illinois, asked 1,079 teenage girls and 921 teenage boys about their influence on various family purchases. Over half of the girls said they buy weekly groceries for the family. About one-quarter of them (24 percent) said that when they shop, they make most of the decisions. Changing family structures mean the main decision maker for many product categories has also changed. The family marketer whose product was mom's favorite must find ways to convince her to impress that preference on her daughter. The family marketer whose product is new in the market can gain a foothold by finding out what appeals to teenage shoppers.

Men are shopping more too, even if only to buy their own neckties. A 1988 survey of American men, sponsored by *GQ* magazine, found a 20 percent drop in the number of ties bought for men by women. Men are also doing more household grocery shopping. Both a poll by Maritz and another conducted for *Men's Health* magazine found that about one-third of men did most or all of the household food shopping. A *GQ* survey found that 51 percent of men had bought household goods like sheets and towels in the past three years, and more than two in five (41 percent) had bought cookware. Being relative newcomers to some of these product categories, men could be more likely than women to accept marketing direction.

While men today are malleable with respect to shopping patterns, both men and women relearn these habits when they first set up housekeeping patterns together. Individual preferences must suddenly be negotiated with another person. Couples quickly discover that there are very few areas where they care equally about the decision. The distribution of decisionmaking tends to become more specialized as the honeymoon ends for newlyweds. In blended families, the period of task-sorting following the remarriage could be shorter because both partners already know their own areas of decisionmaking interest and disinterest.

Many studies have looked at the impact of the wife's work status on family decisionmaking. This impact is smaller than most researchers expected. Just because she has a job, she does not necessarily gain decisionmaking influence. Married women who work at low-paying jobs do not automatically have more influence than nonworking women. What really counts is how much money the wife makes when she works. The more money she brings into the household, or could potentially bring into the household, the more influence she has in family negotiations. Money talks, even at home.

To use the family marketing model, you have to ask a lot of questions and develop appropriate marketing tactics. Like a playwright, you put together characters, plots, and motives. And like a director, you combine technical craftsmanship with creativity. With well-crafted and well-timed marketing tactics, the marketer steps into crucial scenes in the family script and influences the action.

REFERENCES

Abelson, Robert. "Psychological Status of the Script Concept." *American Psychologist,* Vol. 36, No. 7, 1981, pp. 715-729.

Bell, Chip R. and Ron Zemke. *Managing Knock Your Socks Off Service.* New York, NY: AMACOM, 1992.

Corfman, Kim P. and Donald R. Lehmann. "Models of Cooperative Group Decision-Making and Relative Influence: An Experimental Investigation of Family Purchase Decision. *Journal of Consumer Research,* No. 14, June 1987, pp. 1-13.

Crispell, Diane. "The Brave New World of Men," *American Demographics,* January 1992, p. 38.

Davis, Harry L. and Benny P. Rigaux. "Perception of Marital Roles in Decision Processes." *Journal of Consumer Research,* No. 1, June 1974, pp. 51-62.

"Family Cruises Catching On." *Financial Post,* September 16, 1991, p. 44.

Ferber, Robert and Lucy Lee. "Husband-Wife Influence in Family Purchasing Behavior." *Journal of Consumer Research,* No. 1, June 1974, pp. 43-50.

Foxman, Ellen R., Patriya S. Tansuhaj, and Karin M. Ekstrom. "Family Members' Perceptions of Adolescents' Influence in Family Decision Making." *Journal of Consumer Research,* No. 15, March 1989, pp. 482-491.

GQ. *The American Male Opinion Index, Part I.* New York, NY: Condé Nast Publications, Inc., 1988.

Mahatoo, Winston. *The Dynamics of Consumer Behavior.* Toronto, ON: John Wiley & Sons, 1985.

REFERENCES

Marketing News, "If Both Parents Are Breadwinners, Teenagers Often Are the Bread Buyers," Vol. 21, February 13, 1987, p.5.

McNeal, James U. *Kids As Customers.* Lexington, MA: Lexington Books, 1992.

McNeal, James U. "The Littlest Shoppers," *American Demographics,* February 1992, pp. 48-53.

Menasco, Michael B. and David J. Curry. "Utility and Choice: An Empirical Study of Wife/Husband Decision-Making." *Journal of Consumer Research,* No. 16, June 1989, pp. 87-97.

Nett, Emily M. *Canadian Families: Past and Present.* Toronto, ON: Butterworths, 1988, p. 224.

Rubin, Rose M., Bobye J. Riney, and David J. Molina. "Expenditure Pattern Differentials Between One-Earner and Dual-Earner Households: 1972-1973 and 1984." *Journal of Consumer Research,* No. 17, June 1990, pp. 43-52.

Scanzoni, John. "Changing Sex Roles and Emerging Directions in Family Decision Making." *Journal of Consumer Research,* No. 4, December 1977, pp. 185-188.

Schutz, William. *FIRO: A Three-Dimensional Theory of Interpersonal Behavior.* New York, NY: Rinehart, 1958.

Schutz, William. *JOY: Expanding Human Awareness.* New York, NY: Grove Press, 1967.

CHAPTER EIGHT

Family Marketing Research Methods

Individual marketing research treats all respondents as equal carriers of the decisionmaking dynamic at play in the marketplace. At the very least, it assumes that the interpersonal dynamics can be reconstructed from reports given by isolated family members. Family marketing, by contrast, seeks to understand the intimate ways people in a family typically interact when dealing with a product or purchase in what could be called "intimate research." The standard practice of focus group recruitment illustrates the difference. Individual-oriented research requires that no two respondents in a focus group have a prior relationship, because their previous history might influence their responses. In contrast, in family marketing you want people who know each other, and in fact, you want them to be relatives, even if they don't live in the same household, because the direct and indirect ways they influence one another are what you want to observe and understand.

Finding Family Samples

The first step in marketing research is finding people to do research on. Desktop marketing is revolutionizing this process. The hardware and software, however, are following rather than leading. The elements driving these changes are information collection and storage. Large lists and databases are making new approaches and techniques possible, and their greatest impact is in the area of sampling.

Before large lists and databases were available, researchers tried to avoid applying too many qualifications to their samples. The greater the number of screening criteria, the longer it took to find a qualified respondent. Multiple selection criteria were expensive.

> ### ▶ Bigger and Cheaper
>
> Sampling costs are declining. Large databases contain millions of potential respondents nationwide, correlated with dozens of demographic and lifestyle variables.

Today, the sampling costs are declining. Researchers can narrowly target samples because they can find qualifying respondents more quickly. Many large databases contain millions of potential respondents nationwide, correlated with dozens of demographic and lifestyle variables. The demographic and lifestyle variables can be simultaneously applied to identify everyone in the database who meets multiple criteria (e.g., 18-to-21-year-old, part-time employed females who live with their parents and have bought airline tickets in the past six months). From the larger databases, researchers can select a random list of names and telephone numbers of qualifying individuals to contact for research participation.

Database sampling offers promise for researchers in family marketing. List developers must become aware of family marketers' need for lists with more information about family relations among individuals in households and across households. For example, many family-marketing applications could use a good list of grandparents with the ages of their grandchildren.

While such databases are being generated, family marketers can zero in on households of particular types by recruiting from neighborhoods in which they are over-represented. Census data contain such information, and various mapping software packages can make this information easily and cheaply accessible. Once a high-probability neighborhood has been identified, recruitment proceeds randomly until the quota of qualifying households has been met.

Ten years ago, large surveys with multiple screeners based on household composition would have been expensive. Random calling would have included too many neighborhoods with too few qualifying respondents. Today, a family marketing approach no longer faces that barrier. Technology that was originally developed with direct marketing and retail siting applications in mind can now also be used to make recruiting by household composition easy and efficient. *American Demographics* magazine publishes an annual directory of suppliers of such technology.

Interviewing: New Ways to Study Relationships and Interactions

In relationships, it is common for husbands, wives, and children to have different perceptions of who does what, and who has how much influence. In 1981, opinion polls showed that men perceived themselves as more helpful with housework than women thought they were. In a 1989 study, adolescents perceived themselves as having more influence on a variety of purchases than their parents felt they had. Researchers who rely solely on verbal reports from individual respondents are prone to one-sided, inaccurate findings.

Two decades ago, John Scanzoni, a prominent consumer sociologist, warned that capturing information from all involved family members was essential in understanding purchase decisionmaking, but lamented the absence of techniques for making it easier. Recent advances in several areas have made such techniques available.

Current marketing research findings are based almost entirely on what indi-

> **▶ Watch What They Do**
>
> Little research is based on what people actually do. Yet time and time again, the gap between what respondents say and what they do gets marketers in trouble.

vidual respondents say. Very few are based on what these respondents do. Yet time and time again, the gap between what respondents say and what they do gets marketers in trouble.

People usually distort their verbal reports in the directions they feel are more socially desirable. They want to meet the behavioral expectations of the community and to appear to be following current social ideals. In an interview for *Marketing News*, Professor William Rathje of Arizona State University reported that his studies of people's garbage reveal many such inconsistencies. People eat more beef than they say they do and waste more food than they say they eat. They eat less of the healthy foods than they claim to.

When they report on their decisionmaking processes, people are really telling us about their relationships. Relationships, especially family relationships, are often influenced by social ideals and community expectations and are, therefore, prone to distortion. For this reason, good family marketing research, whenever possible, also includes elements of behavioral observation. This may mean looking at the effects of interpersonal behavior patterns, such as the number and condition of children's books in a household where none of the children have yet learned to read, or watching interpersonal behaviors as they happen, such as a mother and teenage daughter buying cranberry sauce for Thanksgiving dinner.

Techniques for watching and analyzing what people do have become more numerous, efficient, and precise. The marketing research industry seems on the verge of adopting some of these as standard practice for individual-oriented research. Behavior observations are even more important and revealing in family marketing. If these become commonly available from research suppliers, it will be a boon to family marketers.

Watching Real-Life Families

Ethnography is what Margaret Mead did when she went to live with the Samoans. She was interested in understanding the world view of a particular segment of society, and to that end, "lived with the tribe."

In the case of families, an ethnographic approach takes the researcher into the family home as an observer. In Britain, ethnographer Arlene Vetere lived with several families and, with co-author Anthony Gale, reported her findings in the book *Ecological Studies of Family Life*. This type of research can obtain real-life observations of how families make many kinds of purchase decisions. The researcher participates in family activities but in every situation takes the role of passive observer. Observations from decisionmaking episodes and from incidents of product purchase, usage, and evaluation are recorded on audiotape at intervals during the day.

Marketing researchers are finding value in ethnographic approaches. For example, Susan Wurtzel of Young and Rubicam reported a study in which researchers interviewed teenagers and spent half a day in their homes with a video camera. Recording things like what was in the cupboards and what posters were on the walls of teens' bedrooms provided enormous insights, especially when combined with focus-group findings.

▶ **Up Close and Personal**

An ethnographic approach takes the researcher into the family home. This type of research can obtain real-life observations of how families make many kinds of purchase decisions.

Ethnographic purists do not feel compelled to make comparisons across "tribes." Marketing researchers, however, often do so if it suits their purposes. If you were interested in how the need for "convenience" translates into the daily lives of single parents versus dual-income parents, ethnography could provide insights. An ethnographer might live with each of ten dual-income families for three days and then live with ten single-parent families for the same amount of time. The last evening of each home visit could be dedicated to a more structured data-collection session.

Observation in the home does not guarantee that a purchase decision about the product category of interest will be made during the ethnographer's visit. But families make purchase decisions or take significant steps toward decisions at predictable places and times in car showrooms and retail environments, for example. In such settings, researchers can use direct observation to more product-specific ends. Furthermore, they can observe dozens of families at once.

Direct behavioral observation can reveal aspects of the interaction that might be omitted from verbal reports. For example, a failed influence attempt from a child to a parent might not be mentioned when family members recount the steps in the decisionmaking process. They might assume that because the influence attempt was unsuccessful, the researcher is not interested in it, or they might simply forget about it. Direct observation of several interactions can improve the way one asks questions.

Not long ago, indoor video recording of family interactions required additional lighting. This was an impediment to in-home videotaping, because it was a constant reminder that the camera was rolling. With advances in video-camera technology, researchers can record direct observations almost anywhere. Today's cameras are much less obtrusive and permit more naturalistic videotaping of in-home behavior.

Once you have captured family interactions, you have to make sense of them. The options range from unstructured viewing to complex coding and analysis systems. Most recent advances have been in the latter area, particularly in techniques for uncovering influences one person might have on another's behavior during an interaction.

Analyzing family behavior sequences begins by "coding" behaviors. Numerous coding systems exist, and it is fairly easy to develop new ones to meet the customized needs of a particular study. Consumer psychology experts have classified coding systems for interactions along two main axes. Such systems can either note or ignore the *duration* and the *sequence* of events.

If the coding system notes the sequence of events, it can reveal patterns indicating one family member's influence on another. For example, if the person playing the role of the family financial officer (FFO) objects to a purchase, the purchase might be postponed in 90 percent of the observed interactions. This suggests but does not prove a causal link between the two events.

If the coding system ignores sequence, analyses usually focus

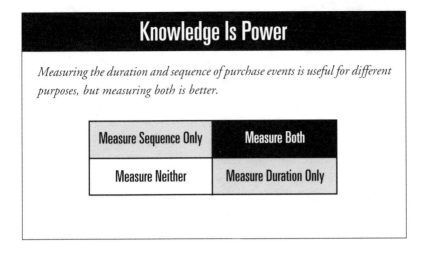

Knowledge Is Power

Measuring the duration and sequence of purchase events is useful for different purposes, but measuring both is better.

Measure Sequence Only	Measure Both
Measure Neither	Measure Duration Only

on how the characteristics of the situation or participants relate to each kind of behavior observed. If one family member plays the expert role because of more comprehensive product knowledge, the other decision makers might limit their remarks to benefit-related questions. If the teenage son is the family expert on video games, the parent and younger sibling involved in the purchase might only ask which is more entertaining or educational. Coding systems that measure the duration of various behaviors can capture more subtle regularities related to the timing of certain events. This tends to be important in face-to-face sales. (For technical information about analyzing coded interaction data, see the Danny Moore reference cited on page 127.)

Simulating the Decision Making Process

Direct observation is less practical when relevant interactions take place over several time periods or across different locations. Bigger decisions tend to take place over long time periods, and events contributing to the decision may take place at unpredictable times and places. For example, a family trying to decide which college a daughter should attend might begin discussing the matter in a hypothetical way before she is even born. By the time high school graduation approaches, the parents and daughter are likely to visit various colleges and discuss their impressions. The exact time and place of these events may not be predictable. The natural decisionmaking process, therefore, cannot be captured on videotape, except by chance.

Script analysis offers an alternative for such situations. A simple method of eliciting scripts was invented in 1985 by sociologists John Pryor and Thomas Merluzzi for their study of dating among college students. They began by asking students to write down 20 actions or events that occur when a male and a female go on a first date. For instance, the most frequently mentioned event (71 percent) was the goodnight kiss.

Later, other students were given the steps in the script and asked to rate how necessary each step was. More frequently mentioned steps were rated as more necessary. A third set of students grouped the script into its "natural parts." The researchers found substantial agreement about how the steps should be grouped into larger "acts" in the script.

Marketing researchers can use the same approach to understand how families decide to buy particular products. From my experience with this approach, people generally begin with large steps. They mention the major "acts" in the decisionmaking process and perhaps a few quirky particulars from a recent experience. Pryor and Merluzzi avoided this kind of general response by asking at the outset for 20 steps. Another option is to write each of the principal acts on an index card, then ask respondents to describe the constituent scenes or substeps involved in each main act and write the scenes on index cards. If necessary, one can repeat the process for each scene. The goal is to provide sufficient detail to capture all family influences on the decisionmaking process. The interviewer must judge when further questioning would yield only irrelevant details.

Script analysis provides a subjective account of how families make purchase decisions. In the process, it identifies the roles played by various family members. It might reveal that most dual-income families start making summer vacation plans when relatives come home from Christmas holidays and talk about those trips. That information could provide guidance for timing vacation travel advertising.

Having collected scripts from each family member, the researcher can look for similarities and differences among them. It is natural for people to generate more scenes for acts in which they were more involved. Keep the following questions in mind while making comparisons:

■ Did everyone agree on the principal acts in the script? How many such acts did they agree on? Did everyone who discussed the decision agree on the number of consultations?

■ Which family members were party to the decisionmaking? Did they agree on who was involved? If not, who left out whom? Did everyone agree on each other's motives?

■ Did conflicting preferences arise during the process? If so, did a true conflict occur? Was there a compromise? Did one person take primary responsibility for solving the conflict?

The final step in script analysis is to compile the results from a substantial number of interviews. Identify the acts and scenes of the composite script. Husbands' scripts can be compared with wives', children's with parents', and those of high-income families with those of low-income families. In general, a difference in scripts indicates a need for a different marketing strategy.

Comparative Critical Incidents

The critical-incident technique is qualitative and exploratory. It offers a "quick and dirty" way to get the perceptions of family members about all or part of the decisionmaking process.

The critical-incident technique involves asking a respondent to recount what happened when a remarkable incident or event of a particular type took place. The respondent might describe the best customer service they ever got from a financial institution or the time they got the best value in a furniture purchase. The response might also describe the first time something happened or the last time something changed.

Such reports from respondents can add flesh-and-blood detail to crucial steps in a purchase decisionmaking script. For example, one might ask, "The first time you thought the family should move

> ## ▶ Verify Reports

> Never assume that the incident happened exactly as reported. Direct behavior observation and the reports of other family members involved can shed light on which areas may have been forgotten or distorted.

the checking account to a different bank, what happened to make you consider the switch?"

Reports obtained through the critical-incident technique are subject to selective memory and memory distortions. Never assume that the incident happened exactly as reported. Direct behavior observation and the reports of other family members involved can shed light on which areas may have been forgotten or distorted.

Comparative Laddering

Many marketing researchers already have a good idea of who potential customers are. They want to know how the product ties into family values of various consumer segments. The best way to answer that question is with a personal interview technique known as laddering. Laddering seems to satisfy the demands that advertising creatives have for insight into what makes consumers tick.

Laddering asks people why they prefer one brand or choice over another, why that option is better, and why it is important. The process is iterated until the respondent answers in terms of basic and deeply held personal values. This technique can reveal how brands are associated with the satisfaction of different values.

Laddering can compare values and perceptions across family members. Some brands may be chosen because they represent a compromise among divergent values. For some product categories, it may even be possible to segment families on the basis of the values they associate with different brands.

Family Decision Simulation

For some products, it is feasible to ask families to make a purchase decision on the spot. Families can be asked to simulate their decisionmaking process so that researchers can observe it. Ideally, a simulation should take place in the setting where the family normally makes such decisions, and be videotaped. The family should set time aside for the simulation to avoid distractions. The simulation will be more realistic if there are valuable incentives, ideally, brands from the product category itself. This is not practical for some categories (e.g., cars), but often product-related incentives can be substituted (e.g., choice of $500 cash rebate on a car purchase or $100 cash). The sampling requirements are similar to those for script analysis.

Play back the videotape of the simulation to the family and ask them to provide additional commentary on what they were thinking or trying to accomplish at various points in the simulation. This can help with coding the videotape. Also, ask the family members to locate the natural break points between the principal acts in the episode they enacted. This helps researchers define the main acts in the decisionmaking script.

Simulations have the strong advantage of being amenable to scheduling. When researchers are interested in the effects that different marketing strategies (e.g., positionings) or tactics (e.g., ads, product prices) have on family decisions, simulations can introduce different options into the decisionmaking process. In this sense, family decisionmaking simulations are the family equivalent of individual-oriented focus groups or taste tests.

If the simulated decision is one that normally takes place over days or weeks, however, one cannot observe the effects of the normal incubation period for perceptions and preferences. When people are forced to compress their decisionmaking, they may weight information, including the preferences of other family members, differently.

When the simulated decision concerns a large-ticket item or otherwise very important purchase (e.g., a house, or vacation), a simulation may not create the same level of arousal that occurs in the natural setting. Arousal and involvement can alter which information is used and how. This is a potential problem. Normally, however, an effective simulation procedure involves most people in the task, even if the stakes are not as high as they would be in real life.

The most serious problem with simulation is that people try to look good in front of the camera. Embedding the simulation in a longer session that gives families plenty of time to get used to the camera may alleviate, but not eliminate, this bias. Families will still tend to make their decisions in ways they perceive to be more socially desirable or politically correct. To look "democratic," for example, they may involve the children more in a simulated decision than they would in a natural setting.

▶ **Playing Pretend**

To overcome the bias of a simulated purchase decision, combine this method with other observation and research.

Most of the disadvantages of simulation can be addressed by using this technique in conjunction with others. Family decisionmaking simulation is best used with techniques that ask families to report how they make decisions (e.g., critical incident, script analysis, direct questioning in a personal interview) and that catch them in the act of making a decision (e.g., direct observation, ethnography). Self reports provide useful information about objective aspects of the naturally occurring decisionmaking process, such as the normal duration, place, and frequency of such decisions. Direct observation and ethnography can bypass the social distortions caused by wanting to look socially correct.

Network Analysis

Network analysis is yet another way to learn about family interactions. It involves looking at who is connected to whom. In their 1982 book *Network Analysis,* David Knoke and James Kuklinski outline seven different possible types of relations among the members of a network:

1. Transaction relations (e.g., buying and selling, gift giving)
2. Communications relations (e.g., who talks to whom, how often)
3. Boundary penetration relations (e.g., membership in multiple families)
4. Instrumental relations (e.g., seeking advice on a purchase)

5. Sentiment relations (e.g., who likes/dislikes whom)
6. Authority/power relations (e.g., who reports to whom)
7. Kinship relations (e.g., who is related to whom)

Any single study might look at two or more kinds of relations. For example, members of a family might be asked about who they are related to (7) and who within their family they would ask for advice when looking for a lawyer (4).

Network analysis has two major applications to family marketing. First, it can be used to plan and evaluate intrafamilial word-of-mouth advertising campaigns. Second, it can help determine the level of family penetration a product has achieved.

Perhaps the most powerful kind of advertising occurs when family members recommend a product to one another. This often happens when one family member actively seeks help or advice from another. Network analysis can identify regular patterns of help- or advice-seeking within families or within certain types of families. For example, to whom do single mothers turn for help when a household appliance fails? Network analysis can identify the characteristics of the most common help-givers. Appliance manufacturers could then examine the benefits of positioning their company to exhibit those characteristics.

Word-of-mouth advertising also occurs in families when someone has an unusual experience with a product or service, especially if it is very good or very bad. In such cases, family members volunteer their evaluations to one another. A family member might talk to one relative when seeking product advice and a different relative when evaluating a brand in that product category. Family members who are told about poor service at a particular hospital, for example, might be different from those whose advice is sought when a child suddenly gets a fever in the middle of the night.

> ▶ **Connections**

Network analysis can be used to plan and evaluate intrafamilial word-of-mouth advertising campaigns and help determine the level of family penetration a product has achieved.

A common family-marketing strategy involves having family members recruit other family members as customers. For example, a bank might reward depositors if all members of their household have accounts there. Network analysis can evaluate the success of such a strategy by estimating the size and composition of customer households and calculating the percentage of eligible family members who became customers.

A variation of this recruitment strategy involves having sets of relatives cooperate in a purchase. Network analysis can help identify optimal groups. For example, a simple form of network analysis can help determine which grandparent (e.g., maternal grandmother) is the best target for promotions that position products as gifts for grandchildren. (For more information about networks, see the citations for Knoke and Kuklinski and for Peter Marsden and Nan Lin on page 127.)

Family Segmentation Systems

Marketing researchers often segment markets into aggregations of consumers who want different things from their products. The key to successful segmentation is to ground it in information about how the consumer relates to the product. Marketers in different product categories, therefore, need different segmentation systems.

An important step in developing a segmentation system is searching for a set of differentiating variables. Several classification schemes differentiate among families, but because they are not tied to specific product categories, they are not adequate as segmentation systems in themselves. When combined with product variables, however, they can often enhance a set of segmentation questions.

Perhaps the oldest scheme for classifying families is the familiar concept of lifestage marketing. In the not-too-distant past, lifestages outlined in typical consumer psychology textbooks were accepted as the norm, even if they never really reflected more than an aspiration or social expectation. Childhood is the first lifestage. Children affect their parents' purchase decisions and priorities. Proceeding chronologically, the consumption patterns and influences of teenagers come next. Then, people enter young adulthood and focus on finding a mate and starting a family. Parents of school-age children are sometimes noted as a distinct stage, and parents of teens have always faced unique challenges. The empty-nester stage comes after the children leave but before retirement. Early retirement is distinct from the later years, and old age is usually marked by debilitating decline in health and/or widowhood.

This familiar sequence is inadequate to describe the diversity that actually exists. It is not unusual for people to form new households and start new families two or three times during their lives. Parents with young children might be in their 50s, when one might expect them to be empty nesters. Others in their 50s could be early retirees, and people in their 70s are decreasingly likely to have the poor health and/or widowhood characteristics associated with old age.

The general concept of lifestage is nonetheless still useful if one assumes less about the nature of families in any given lifestage; the sequencing of the stages, especially in midlife; and the number of lifestages any one individual experiences. For many, remarriage creates a "second family" stage. Likewise, many parents enter an "adult student" or "second career" stage when their children get a little older.

Some systems for classifying families focus on how the family faces the balance between job and home. One of the older systems of this type, described by Walters in 1978, placed families into four categories. In the "career-oriented" family, job requirements took precedence in many family decisions. The "consumption-oriented" family placed more importance on the owning of material possessions. The "family-oriented" or "child-oriented" family placed more importance on family togetherness, and the "socially oriented" family emphasized participation in social events and having active social lives.

> ▶ **Lifestages Revisited**
>
> The familiar sequence of childhood to adolescence through family formation, empty nest, and retirement is inadequate to describe the diversity that exists today, but the general concept of lifestage is still useful.

Since women entered the work force in large numbers, more recent systems have emphasized the wife's income-earning role. Rosemary Polegato developed a system with three categories for wives' job orientations—career, income, and nonworking—and two for husbands' job orientations—career and income. The system successfully predicts women's usage of labor- or time-saving food preparation strategies.

> ## ▶ Across the Board
>
> A family marketing approach offers the promise of appealing to several segments at once. By selling to entire families, a marketer can deepen penetration into segments that would otherwise be inaccessible.

Classification systems for families that do not relate to product categories can still be useful because they were developed with novel data collection and statistical techniques that marketing researchers can also use. Thomas Draper and Anastasios Marcos have compiled a book that describes several innovative techniques for classifying families.

Classifying families into product-relevant segments works best for families living in the same household. When other relatives are included, the resulting diversity might make segmentation meaningless, and marketers might better look at strategies that allow them to target several segments at once.

A family marketing approach offers the promise of appealing to several segments at once. Most families contain representatives of two or three individual-based segments. Husbands and wives are most likely to be in the same individual psychographic segment. People tend to marry those like themselves, and married people tend to reinforce their spouses similarly. Across generations and across households, however, the probability of family members being in different segments is higher. By selling to entire families, a marketer can deepen penetration into segments that would otherwise be inaccessible.

For some brands, the niche strategy of targeting single segments has become a self-imposed straitjacket. Market segmentation has made it possible for marketers to design and position their products in a way that better matches consumers' needs. In some product categories, however, efforts to offer something to every segment have led to product proliferation, which in turn creates advertising clutter. Family marketing can help break out of narrowly defined segments.

REFERENCES

Bakeman, R. "Untangling the Streams of Behavior." *Observing Behavior Volume II: Data Collection and Analysis Methods.* Sackett, G.P., editor. Baltimore, MD: University Park Press, 1978.

Draper, Thomas W. and Anastasio C. Marcos, editors. *Family Variables: Concepualizations, Measurement and Use.* Newbury Park, CA: Sage Publications, 1990.

Foxman, Ellen R., Patriya S. Tansuhaj, and Karin M. Ekstrom. "Family Members' Perceptions of Adolescents' Influence in Family Decision Making." *Journal of Consumer Research,* No. 15, March 1989, pp. 482-491.

Knoke, David and James H. Kuklinski. *Network Analysis.* Beverly Hills, CA: Sage Publications, 1982.

Marsden, Peter and Nan Lin, editors. *Social Structure and Network Analysis.* Beverly Hills, CA: Sage Publications, 1982.

Miller, Robert. "Charting New Ground for Segmentation." *Bank Marketing,* May 1991, p. 44.

Moore, Danny L. "Social Interaction Data: Procedural and Analytic Strategies." *Perspectives on Methodology in Consumer Research.* Brinberg, David and Richard Lutz, editors. New York: Springer-Verlag, 1986, pp. 181-209.

Nett, Emily M. *Canadian Families: Past and Present.* Toronto, ON: Butterworths, 1988, p. 222.

Olson, Jerry C. and Thomas J. Reynolds. "Understanding Consumers' Cognitive Structures: Implications for Advertising Strategy." *Advertising and Consumer Psychology.* Lexington, MA: Lexington Books, 1983, pp. 77-90.

REFERENCES

Polegato, Rosemary. *The Relevance of a Behavioural Family Structure Variable in Segmentation of a Family Market.* Ph.D dissertation, Faculty of Graduate Studies, University of Western Ontario, Canada, 1986.

Pryor, John B. and Thomas V. Merluzzi. "The Role of Expertise in Processing Social Interaction Scripts." *Journal of Experimental Social Psychology, 21,* 1985, pp. 362-379.

Reynolds, Thomas and Jonathan Gutman. "Laddering Theory, Method, Analysis, and Interpretation." *Journal of Advertising Research,* February/March 1988, pp. 11-31.

Schlosberg, Jeremy. "Stalking the Elusive Grandparent." *American Demographics,* July 1990, p. 32.

Vetere, Arlene and Anthony Gale. *Ecological Studies of Family Life.* New York: John Wiley & Sons, 1987.

Walters, C. Glenn. *Consumer Behavior—Theory and Practice.* Homewood, IL: Richard D. Irwin, 1978.

Wurtzel, Susan. presentation given to the Advertising Research Foundation, July 23, 1992, cited by Breedon, Brenda. "Qualitative Research: Where We Are and Where We're Going." *Imprint: PMRS Newsletter,* October 1992, p. 6.

CHAPTER NINE

The Four P's of Family Marketing

Understanding the principles of family marketing allows you to view traditional marketing strategies in a new light. Any introductory marketing textbook explains the "four P's" of marketing, but a family marketing perspective expands their meaning.

The four P's of marketing are price, product, place, and promotion. "Price" covers the many types of analyses and strategies related to pricing a product or service. "Product" includes everything from the physical aspects of what you are selling to nebulous concepts like brand equity. "Place" refers to where or how the product is sold and includes all issues related to distribution. "Promotion" covers product communications, including advertising, promotions, and unpaid media coverage.

The four P's represent the fundamentals of marketing. In family marketing, they take new twists and extend our strategic horizons in new directions. Without consciously setting out to do "family marketing," many marketers have successfully implemented family-marketing principles in one or two areas. Others have been more deliberate. This chapter looks at those who have succeeded in the effort.

Price

Families sometimes have an advantage over individuals in the marketplace because they can pool their buying power. For product categories in which the packaging cost or other sales costs are relatively high, the bulk-buying capacity of families can be leveraged into a cost savings for consumers. Offering a "family package" or "family size" is a good way to deliver value.

The trend in recent decades has been away from family packages toward individual packages. Individual packages can be more profitable per unit, especially in a time when household size is declining and the standard of living is rising. It was during just such a period that Japanese and other foreign-car manufacturers gained market share in North America by offering low-cost subcompact cars. Nuclear families with several children did not buy them, but those larger households were disappearing then, anyway.

Now that the era of the ever-shrinking household may be drawing to a close, marketers could find an advantage in returning to family-size packages. Family packages do not have to cannibalize the individual packages in one's own product line. If the typical household uses a combination of a competitor's individual packages and yours, the company that adds family packages will gain market share. This is what American car manufacturers have managed to do with minivans. Sales of "family-size" passenger vehicles like station wagons and minivans have risen with the advent of the parent boom. In one telling ad, Chrysler shows a family that "five years ago had so many Hondas that Honda actually made a commercial about them." Now they have a single Chrysler minivan. Chrysler took customers away from Honda by offering a family-size product.

Product pricing is often used to encourage trial or patronage. Such strategies take on a new twist in a family-marketing

▶ **War Stories**

Learn how marketers have succeeded in marketing to families using the four "P's:" price, product, place, and promotion.

context. Consider the "Family Ties" mortgage offered by Canada Trust, a 330-branch financial institution in Canada. The Family Ties mortgage involves older parents and their adult children, and it appeals to parents who want to help their children but do not want to go into the mortgage business with their retirement savings. The children get a regular mortgage, but the interest rate is lower, and the amount of the reduction balances the lower rate the parents decide to accept on a term deposit (i.e., the equivalent of a certificate of deposit). If the parents deposit $50,000 at a rate 2 percent below the current rate, the children get $50,000 of their mortgage at 2 percent below the current mortgage rate. Meanwhile, Canada Trust gains two new customers perfectly matched as borrowers and lenders.

In the United States, Merrill Lynch developed the Parent Power program to encourage parents to help their adult children buy homes. The parents pledge assets to provide the equivalent of a downpayment for their children and avoid depleting their brokerage accounts and paying capital-gains taxes. Meanwhile, the children can get into a home without a downpayment. Merrill Lynch keeps the parents' business while gaining the children as borrowing customers.

The United Savings Bank in San Francisco offered price breaks like free checking to families with a combined balance of more than $10,000. A family included all related people living at the same address. Since their primary customer base was the Asian community in San Francisco, many households included two generations of adults. The year this family promotion was introduced, their deposits grew by 22 percent. Profits rose by about the same percentage.

Charles Kwan, a vice president at United Savings, explained that family pricing has evolved through three stages. First was account-level pricing. Every account had a schedule of interest rates and service charges. Next came relationship pricing. Every customer's total relationship with the bank, in terms of deposits and loans,

> ## ▶ Bulk Is Back
>
> Now that the era of the ever-shrinking household may be drawing to a close, marketers could find an advantage in returning to family-size packages.

was taken into account in setting prices. Third, family-level pricing evolved when banks gained the ability to set prices according to the total funds (i.e., deposit and/or loan balance) deposited by a group of people.

While the definition of "family" used by the United Savings Bank works well with an Asian clientele, other market segments might prefer a looser definition. Royal Trust, a mid-sized financial institution based in Toronto, generalized the concept of family pricing into what might better be described as "multiperson relationship pricing."

Royal Trust's Alliance Program bases prices on a designated group of demand deposit accounts, called an "alliance." Customers take the initiative in applying to form an alliance, members of which do not have to be related or live at the same address. Examples of alliances include family members living in different cities, gay couples, or even members of a baseball team.

When the average balance exceeds a certain threshold, everyone in the alliance is spared service charges on several types of transactions. When the average falls below this threshold, only members whose accounts are below that level have to pay service charges for that month. Senior members of the group and people with balances over $60,000 receive additional interest on deposits.

Although the Alliance Program is not restricted to families, it is ideal for family use. One newspaper ad described how, with his high balance, grandfather graciously ensures that the alliance's average balance will always be above that required for free transactions. Who knows where grandfather had his money before the alliance was formed? If it was at another institution, then Royal Trust gained a large deposit at a low cost. If it was in a Royal Trust deposit bearing higher interest, then Royal Trust got a discount on the deposit.

Product

If the purchase decision for your product involves family more than you had previously realized, can you appeal to additional family members? One marketer able to say "yes" to this question was Regent Holidays, a tour operator based in Mississauga, Ontario,

Canada. From a survey of passengers, it discovered that as many as 27 percent of summer holiday trips to the sunny south were based on family decisions influenced by children. In looking more closely at the role of children in vacation decisionmaking, it concluded that satisfaction with the children's programs included in holiday packages is extremely important. This led Regent Holidays to launch its Junior Good Times Club.

Phil Egan, Regent's marketing manager, emphasizes that the club is more than glorified babysitting. It gives children a fun-filled program in a flexible schedule so families can have as much time together as they want. The Junior Good Times Club boosted sales so much that Regent later added an additional child-oriented promotion. Regent hopes the positive experience will also generate brand awareness and loyalty that will persist among today's children when they become tomorrow's young-adult travelers and among today's parents when they become tomorrow's empty-nester travelers.

> ▶ **Plural Power**
>
> The United Savings Bank in San Francisco offered price breaks like free checking to families with a combined balance of more than $10,000. The year this promotion was introduced, deposits grew by 22 percent.

Like Regent Holidays, several hotel chains have added features to their products to appeal to additional generations. Hyatt Hotels and Resorts has developed "Camp Hyatt," a national children's program that awards points much like a frequent-flyer program. At each resort, the Camp Hyatt passport entitles children to activities ranging from tennis lessons to waterslides. In Hawaii, resort hotels offer children's programs with features like a free pet gecko, marine-life field trips, photography classes, kite flying, Hawaiian arts and crafts, and field trips galore. The travel industry has enhanced its product to appeal to an additional generation of family decision makers.

If different generations within a family buy products in your category or even just talk to each other about your product category, you should investigate a full lifecycle product range. This means offering a separate product for customers in each lifestage. A single brand ties the product line together.

In financial services, the bank is the brand. Most banks have children's accounts for youngsters, car-loan promotions for young adults, mortgage deals for established adults ready for a home, savings instruments for middle-aged people, and all sorts of perks and bonuses for seniors. The Credit Union National Association and CUNA Mutual Insurance developed the "Marketing & Success Happens" program to show credit unions how to develop and offer products for members at each stage of the lifecycle. Offering something for every generation has two advantages. It lets families resolve generational conflicts over product preferences without having to switch to a competitive supplier or brand. And a cradle-to-grave product line permits lifelong brand loyalty.

▶ Something for Everyone

Offering something for every generation lets families resolve generational conflicts over product preferences and permits lifelong brand loyalty.

A "peacemaking" product achieves a compromise among the divergent tastes of family members that lets them meet their own needs while keeping the others happy at the same time. When family members have different purchase preferences, they normally take turns. Sometimes, however, there is no next time. For example, grandmother only has one 95th birthday dinner. If Aunt Martha gets her choice of restaurant this year, Aunt Mildred might not get her choice next year. If mom gets the car she wants this time, dad might have to wait ten years to get his choice.

When one family member acts as purchasing agent for other family members, that individual often seeks products that satisfy as many as possible of the criteria advocated by different family members. Breakfast-cereal manufacturers have become adept at developing compromise brands that satisfy both parents' nutritional concerns and children's taste and fun criteria.

Likewise, the growing popularity of home fitness equipment might result from the compromise it achieves for dual-income baby boomers. Caught between the time demands of family and fitness, exercising at home instead of at a health club is a compromise solution.

Place

The parent boom has changed shopping and consumption habits. Not only does more consumption take place inside the home, but more shopping happens there, too. Catalog marketers like L. L. Bean and Patagonia have prospered by appealing to the in-home shopper. Direct-mail and telephone advertising has blossomed into a huge industry over the past decade, and TV shopping channels have increased the shop-at-home options.

Putting shopping options into the home works best when you target them. Base your targeting on a solid grasp of the family decisionmaking process. Do specific life events trigger purchases of your products? If so, what kind? A birth, a graduation, a change of residence, a death? Who in the family notices the need first? Who does the shopping? Who influences the purchase decision?

Lists and databases are available for increasing numbers of life events. Direct marketing is more effective when you combine knowledge of the household composition and life-event calendar with an understanding of how families make decisions to buy products in your category.

There is no need to confine lists to single events. David Chambers of Target Marketing Services at Keller Moleski Associates in Kalamazoo, Michigan, finds that most lists contain 60 to 80 percent of the data one needs to perform a lifestage segmentation. A simple segmentation model uses basic variables like income, age of head of household, marital status, renter versus owner, and children by age. Chambers predicts that the demand for lifestage mailing lists will grow, especially as the increasing amounts of information available on lists allow the models to become more sophisticated.

Parallel to the tendency to shop from home is the trend toward home consumption. The boom in at-home entertainment and recreation has also been called "cocooning." Live arts and cultural events are struggling because of reduced attendance. Cocooning often gets the blame. One might speculate that cocooning resulted from shifts in people's values, a back-to-basics movement. A recent survey, however, suggests that cocooning *per se* has a different cause. Decima Research of Toronto and Les Consultants Cultur'inc of Montreal asked 52,000 Canadians how often they go to restaurants, movies, plays, art galleries, museums, and other cultural venues outside the home. Two-thirds said they would like to go out more often. The authors of the report suggest that cocooning is a response to the costs of babysitters and tickets.

> ▶ **Stay-at-Homes**
>
> Cocooning may be a response to the costs of babysitters and tickets. Companies that can deliver their product or service in the home will find a willing market among parents of younger children.

Babysitters tend to be aged 13 to 18. Today's 13-to-18-year-old cohort is part of what demographers call the birth dearth. The ratio of babysitters to parents is low relative to previous decades, and the relative cost of babysitters is, therefore, high. Given that barrier, companies that can deliver their product or service in the home will find a willing market among parents of younger children.

Architects and interior designers have responded to the stay-at-home trend with the "Great Room" concept, a family room connected with the kitchen, a dining area, and so on. Parents can entertain friends while staying in visual contact with the children. IKEA, a Swedish furniture manufacturer, offers designs to furnish this new kind of family entertainment space.

Businesses that depend on customers getting out of the house can entice parents with features and facilities for kids. McKids is just such a store. The result of a licensing agreement between McDonald's and Sears, McKids bills itself as "The Store for Kids." McKids stores feature displays and activities to keep kids amused and make toy shopping less of a burden for parents.

Other retailers are trying to become more child-friendly, too.

"Kids clubs" are springing up everywhere. A National Restaurant Association survey found at least 50 percent of responding restaurants offered anything from a kiddie menu to child care.

Promotion

No one buys anything unless they make a connection between the product and an unmet need or desire. The way to motivate a purchase is to meet the buyer's physical and social needs.

In the developed world, most people's physical needs (e.g., food, clothing, shelter) are satisfied, and they often have choices about how to satisfy those needs. They can use social needs such as love, acceptance, or belonging to make arbitrary decisions, and choose the brand or supplier that satisfies a social need. Any number of automobiles in the same price range could satisfy the need for basic transportation. Appealing to different social needs sets them apart from one another. For example, a Volkswagen ad shows how a young man impresses a young woman with his car, a VW Passat. By contrast, a Toyota Camry TV ad shows a young father using a drive in the car to lull a crying baby to sleep.

Social needs can also be met through services like charities, dating services, or hair stylists. This poses the question, "Which social needs should we associate our product with?"

The short answer is, "The deepest ones that go unfulfilled in the greatest number of people." The deepest social needs all relate to forming and maintaining a family, everything from lust to nurturing. Psychologists who study personality say that the basic personality is formed by the age of 5. It forms in a family context and exerts an emotional and motivational force for years thereafter.

> ▶ **Motivators**
>
> Which social needs should you associate your product with? The deepest ones that go unfulfilled in the greatest number of people.

An ad for mutual funds from Selected Financial Services Inc. shows two young boys swinging over a creek on a tire tied to a rope.

The headline reads, "Jim and Jason would rather Dad concentrate on Wall Creek than on Wall Street." The tag line is, "The feeling is mutual." The ad agency BBDO/Chicago deliberately tried to connect with a neotraditional attitude that disdains rampant materialism and places more importance on human relationships.

> ▶ **Truth in Advertising**
>
> Today, women are more likely to be shown as most of them really are: older and heavier than fashion models. As family marketing evolves, we will likely see more realistic portrayals of families, too.

In order to avoid looking too much like a Norman Rockwell painting for contemporary tastes, many marketers use ads that show family interactions in real-life situations. Kmart of Troy, Michigan, takes this approach in slice-of-life TV ads aimed at baby boomers. Kmart's marketing acknowledges the time poverty that today's families suffer.

In a sense, the portrayal of families in advertising today is where the portrayal of women in advertising was 15 years ago. At that time, the "fashion model" ideal was everywhere in advertising but was deeply resented by real women. Today, women are more likely to be shown as most of them really are: older and heavier than fashion models. As family marketing evolves, we will likely see more realistic portrayals of families, too. Impish boys may get caught poking their brothers during family portraits, and dads may growl while pulling toys out of blocked toilet bowls.

Already, some advertisers are producing ads that acknowledge and deal with changing family structures and roles. For example, Catelli has a TV commercial showing an apparently single mother having dinner with her children. And ads that show men with babies seem to be everywhere. They acknowledge the less rigid assignment of household tasks by gender in today's families. You see the woman's perspective in a recent deodorant ad that showed a woman working as an architect on a big construction job.

It is clearly possible to overdo the baby angle, especially if your

The seeming explosion of kids in advertising was the subject of a Cathy cartoon.

product or service is also purchased by childless people. American Express created a TV ad that might have appealed more to Cathy. The ad deals with the incongruent lifestyles that a mother and her daughter have chosen. The mother probably expected her daughter to get married and raise a family. The daughter seems to have been busy pursuing a career instead. But that means she earns enough to buy her father the more expensive set of golf clubs he would prefer, using her American Express card, of course. Between the lines lies mom's regret at not having had a career herself, balanced by her total commitment to family. The daughter resolves her internal conflict over home versus career by pleasing her parents. But the mother is still proud of her daughter, and the daughter still appreciates her mother's support. And they both want to make dad happy.

This is a good example of how family marketing is not restricted to people living in the same household or to people with children at home. The young woman in this ad could represent the increasing numbers of single-person households, or she might be one of the now more prevalent childless-couple households. But she still has strong feelings about family, feelings you can arouse to get her to listen to your message.

The term "promotion" covers many activities from contests to discounts. These too can be approached from a family-marketing perspective. In 1991, Johnson & Johnson ran an "Adorable Babies" contest. Consumers sent in videos of their kids. The finalists were shown on a television special called "America's Cutest KIDS!" It was billed as "hilarious real-life home-video segments of kids doing some surprising and unexpected things." It gave Johnson & Johnson a chance to present its products and its company to a highly child-oriented audience on a prime-time Sunday night TV broadcast.

Family members often gather in front of the TV set, but there are other viable venues for family promotions. Promotions tied to theme parks, zoos, day-care centers, senior-care homes, and children's events are common at local levels, but because such promotions depend on a family's physical attendance, they are seldom feasible on a regional or national scale.

Family marketing has lent a new twist to trade shows. In October 1992, the first Parents Show took place. Hundreds of companies displayed their wares to parents in Toronto. Exhibitors included Ford, Gerber, and *Today's Parent* magazine. The show's organizer, George Przybylowski of Corporate Events Management, Inc., plans to set up similar events in other cities. The show's manager, Jacqueline

Peake, says it fills a need created by changing family structures. She says the decline of the extended family and the increase in the age of first childbearing mean today's older parents often do not have parents of their own to turn to for support or advice about child-rearing. Even when they do, they may feel that their own parents are out of touch with today's social environment.

Family members talk about more than parenting. Word-of-mouth is crucial for all sorts of products and services. Richmond Savings Credit Union of Richmond, British Columbia, Canada, discovered how important intrafamilial word-of-mouth can be when it compared customer satisfaction ratings with customer recommendations. The credit union asked a randomly selected panel of 27 members if they had ever recommended Richmond Savings to a friend, acquaintance, or relative. It also asked them to rate their satisfaction with the service at Richmond Savings and the service at other financial institutions with which they were familiar.

Those who rated Richmond Savings as superior to another institution were equally likely to have recommended it to relatives, work acquaintances, and friends. Those who thought the service at Richmond Savings was about the same as elsewhere had recommended it to friends and work acquaintances but were significantly less likely to recommend it to relatives. To get its customers to recommend Richmond Savings to other family members, the credit union had to convince the customer that its service was clearly superior.

The point is that customers apply more stringent criteria in making word-of-mouth recommendations within their families. If everyone plays by these rules, it is no wonder that recommendations made by a family member seem more credible than those made by friends or colleagues.

Perhaps the best-promoted family word-of-mouth program was MCI's "Friends & Family," which offered a 20 percent discount on long-distance calling. In the first 14 months of the plan, MCI gained 5 million new customers. AT&T responded with an ad that fought fire with fire. It used family marketing principles against MCI's Friends & Family program. AT&T's ad shows a young man listening to the messages on his answering machine after he has given the names and addresses of friends and family to another long-distance

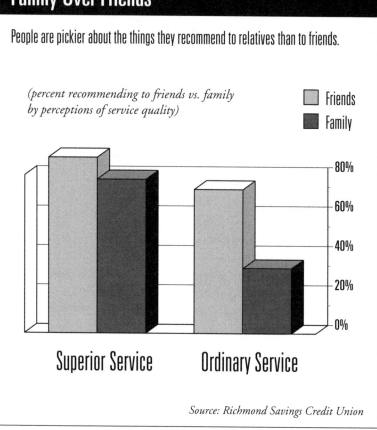

Family Over Friends

People are pickier about the things they recommend to relatives than to friends.

(percent recommending to friends vs. family by perceptions of service quality)

▧ Friends
■ Family

- 80%
- 60%
- 40%
- 20%
- 0%

Superior Service   Ordinary Service

Source: Richmond Savings Credit Union

company. All the messages relay negative reactions. The young man turns off the machine saying, "It's just not worth it." AT&T is reinforcing the principle that word-of-mouth recommendations within families are given carefully and judiciously. Because family relations are so important, reckless recommendations can bring about serious social consequences.

Within-family word-of-mouth campaigns can be powerful marketing tactics. Because they are so powerful, however, they must be used carefully. Marketers must make certain that their current customer base is loyal and highly satisfied. With high customer turnover, this tactic is less likely to work.

REFERENCES

Canadian Press. "Major Study Finds Canadians Want to Be Cultured—If They Can Find a Babysitter." *The Vancouver Sun*, May 30, 1992, p. H3.

"Car Makers Target Families..." *Marketing News, 26*, 10, May 11, 1992, p. 1.

Chambers, David. "Data Technology Boosts Popularity of Lifestage Marketing." *Marketing News*, October 28, 1991, p. 16.

Colemand, Lynn G. "'Right Now, Kids are Very Hot': Retailers Doing All They Can to Grab Them Early and Often." *Marketing News*, June 25, 1990, p. 1.

Egan, Phil. "Targeting Family Travel: A Case Study on the Junior Good Times Club," presentation given at Consumer Kids: How to Grow Your Customers from Childhood, April 29, 1992.

Goerne, Carrie. "Mutual Fund Ads Emphasize Family, Fun." *Marketing News*, May 25, 1992, p. 5.

Hellmich, Nanci. "Travails of Eating Out with the Kids." *USA Today*, September 11, 1992, p. 1D.

Kroll, Barb and Ron Kroll. "Hawaii's Vacation Resorts Now Compete in Catering to the Keikis." *The Vancouver Sun*, January 4, 1992, p. F1.

Miller, Cyndee. "Convenience, Variety Spark Huge Demand for Home Fitness Equipment." *Marketing News*, March 16, 1992, p. 2.

National Credit Union Youth Program. *Marketing and Success Happens*. Madison, WI: CUNA Mutual Insurance Group, 1988.

Schlossberg, Howard. "Kmart's New Approach Aims Straight for the Heart." *Marketing News*, April 1, 1991, p. 8.

Scotland, Randall. "IKEA Eyes Cocooning Set." *The Financial Post*, September 21, 1992, p. 7.

Scotland, Randall. "Real Women Stepping into the Limelight in Advertising." *The Financial Post,* October 8, 1992, p. 15.

Waggoner, John. "Parents Pledge Assets to Help Kids Buy Homes." *USA Today,* March 27, 1992, p. 1B.

■

Chapter Ten

Family Marketing and Social Issues in Advertising

The "me" decade is, if not dead, unwell. People's hot buttons are increasingly family-oriented, and sexual appeals and appeals based on prestige and ostentation are less popular.

Controversies and Family Advertising

Images of the singles' bar lifestyle might still attract young men, but legal challenges and pressure from women's groups make sex appeal risky in advertising. The Stroh Brewery Co., for example, has been sued for sexual harassment by five female employees. Their suit alleges that the company's advertising, including a TV ad depicting a "Swedish bikini team," contributed to harassment on the job. Reacting specifically to beer ads, the Province of Ontario has banned "sexism" in advertising. Because of this bad publicity, beer advertisers are changing their tactics. Michelob has "special occasions" ads that show, among other things, a victorious women's softball team and "the Sullivan sisters" getting together for a beer in Feeney's Pub. The ads have run in *Vogue, Cosmopolitan,* and *Mademoiselle* in an attempt to attract women consumers.

Family advertising might be a little safer, but it is not entirely invulnerable, either. Advertisers would be mistaken to think they can avoid feminist attacks simply by turning to family themes. Depicting women in family roles must be handled carefully. Aprons, for example, can be very inflammatory, unless men wear them. Scenes of husbands leaving for work while wives stay home can also raise feminist objections, especially if the wife seems to enjoy it. Feminists call this "momism" or "Cleaver fever," a reference to June Cleaver, the quintessential stay-at-home mom of the 1950s. So although family theme ads can provide a safe alternative, they can also be as sexist as the Swedish bikini team.

In today's post-Boesky, post-Milken, and post-Savings and Loan scandal atmosphere, ad images of high-flying success are likely to make a product as attractive as J. R. Ewing, the greedy villain of the TV series *Dallas.* Max Blackston of Ogilvy and Mather gives the example of American Express offending potential customers with the high status and prestige "personality" that early ads gave its card. The tone came across as authoritarian to too many potential customers.

This is one advertising problem that family-related themes apparently can solve. Sensing the popular perception that business and unbridled greed are incompatible with a happy, healthy family life, some advertisers have hastily shed success themes in favor of family themes. British Airways, for example, used to run ads that promised to get the business traveler to the big meeting on time. Now it promises to get him home to his wife and children.

In a similar vein, Mercedes-Benz is trying to distance itself from the materialistic image of the 1980s. Its 1992 ads emphasize relationships, especially family relationships. In one, a father gives a Mercedes as a wedding gift. In another, a woman recalls seeing a traffic accident when she was a child. Just as the audience realizes the woman is driving to pick up her own daughter at school, the woman remarks, "No, I don't drive a Mercedes to impress my friends." The appeal to child protection and transgenerational relations is exactly right for today's neotraditional consumer.

Advertising Aimed at Children

Several areas of controversy in advertising concern children in the family—the line between entertainment and advertising, the issue of gender typing, and the relationship between privacy and database marketing.

When children are involved, the context of advertising becomes controversial. Merchandising has blurred the line between cartoon characters and toys. Popular cartoon characters create box-office success, and toy, T-shirt, lunchbox, and many other kinds of sales. Critics argue that the cartoons have become ads in disguise. Disguised advertising is exploitative because it takes advantage of young children's difficulty in distinguishing between fiction and reality.

The debate over gender stereotyping in toys has been around for decades. The latest skirmish involved a Teen Talk Barbie™ doll, who says math is tough. Critics argue that the phrase perpetuates the stereotype that girls cannot do math. Barbie's defenders counter with scientific studies showing that students who think math is easy do worse than those who think it is tough and requires hard work. Unfortunately, the lesson for marketers in this case is that scientific studies do not prevent public attacks. Mattel, Barbie's manufacturer, has been forced to institute a refund policy. Upon request, it will replace any doll that says math is tough with one that does not.

> ▶ **Family Over Job**
>
> British Airways used to run ads that promised to get the business traveler to the big meeting on time. Now it promises to get him home to his wife and children.

Children like to receive mail and might respond to it very well. Their parents, however, might not. Some parents think it is bad enough that their own names sit on a marketer's database and are furious when the same thing happens to their children. They have two principal objections. First, since children are more impressionable, they are more easily exploited by marketers. Many parents want to act as filters between their children and the media to which they are exposed. Second, some fear that the indiscriminate distribution of lists of children could result in kidnapping and abduction.

Family marketers seeking detailed family and household information are well advised to use the principle of informed consent in constructing such databases. The same principle should apply to distributing such information. Moreover, "informed consent" should be taken to mean that the parents consent to specific future uses of family information. For example, if information obtained from entry forms in a contest will be used for a direct-mail campaign, the contest rules should say so. Database- and list-builders may eventually want to consider asking consumers to specifically license future use of their personal information.

Family and Household Diversity in Ads

Family marketing looks at family relationships and how they affect purchase decisions. Changing relationships within families have implications for the marketing of some products. Broadly aimed ads today must recognize diversity more than they did in the past. They have to appeal to people like step-parents who decide what toppings to order on the family pizza and married but deliberately childless women who choose nursing homes for their elderly mothers.

But this is not a limitation; it is an opportunity. Ads that acknowledge and empathize with diverse household and family lifestyles can be more effective than those that do not. The diversity itself can help focus ads on concrete daily situations that contain easily aroused emotions based on family relationships. Link those emotions to the product, and your ad is a winner.

Women and men increasingly influence each other's traditional marketplace turf. For example, 80 percent of car purchases are either made or influenced by women. That is one reason why Mazda has sponsored the *Family Circle* women's tennis tournament and two Ladies Professional Golf Association (LPGA) championships.

A 1992 survey by the Grocery Products Manufacturers of Canada found that 21 percent of all grocery shoppers are men. Contrast this with the 13 percent who were men in 1987. Since they are relatively new to this task, men tend to shop differently than women, i.e., less efficiently. Dave Nichol, president of Loblaw's International Merchants, says, "Men have not spent their lives studying ways to drive supermarkets into bankruptcy." Men are less likely to make lists and compare prices. At the same time, they are less patient with long checkout lines. Women want to save money; men want to save time.

At home, the rise in single-parent households headed by women has left a void in the home-handiness department. More households have no adult male, and more women are facing home repairs and appliance or toy assembly problems. This could create a willing market for extended service and warranty contracts.

Knowing about genders of children in a family can help determine the best strategy for advertising and promotion. For example, families with a father and school-aged boys, but no school-aged girls, are likely to consume certain kinds of sports-related media and messages related to sports such as baseball, basketball, and football. Dan Lipson, president of DSL Communications in New York City, helps companies use sports videos to reach today's media-literate children. Many companies have successfully used National Basketball Association videos as promotional premiums. To take another example, if you know that an identifiable group of households (e.g., a target segment or occasional product-users) has more female teenagers than other households, then you know that a teenager in those households is more likely to do major food and grocery shopping for the family at least once a month.

> ▶ **The Shopping Gender Gap**
>
> Men are less likely to make lists and compare prices. They are less patient with long checkout lines. Women want to save money; men want to save time.

Acknowledging and working with family diversity in ads is part of the larger opportunity of dealing with household diversity. Household diversity means more than just family diversity; it includes gay couples and the growing number of single-person households.

The gay market has a relatively high disposable income and spends generously in certain categories. Marketers trying to appeal to the gay market might assume that they cannot use family marketing, because it would offend their target customers. Such assumptions are based on unthinking stereotypes. The stereotype says that all gays have been rejected by their families, can only find acceptance within the gay community, and do not keep in touch with their parents and siblings. Many gays, however, would like to see that stereotype disappear along with all the rest. The truth is that many gays have supportive families and that many of their relatives would appreciate a supportive marketer as well.

> ## ▶ Consider the "Nonfamily"
>
> Household diversity means more than just family diversity; it includes gay couples and the growing number of single-person households.

Singles might seem the least suitable targets for family marketing. Not so. In a July 1991 article in *Business Week*, Timothy F. Price, senior vice president for marketing at MCI Telecommunications, says, "Single people don't have nuclear families. So they're more emotionally connected to family and friends elsewhere." In fact, single people often carry on a longer, stronger attachment to their parents than those who have married. As a result, ads that acknowledge and appeal to such attachments can be very effective with that audience. If done well, such ads can grab singles' attention and forge emotional links with the product.

The same may be true for single parents. Children of single parents spend more time with their parents' parents and relatives than children in two-parent households. Advertisers who discover that single parents are one of their best target markets can easily put the single-parent message across without making a political moral statement.

Staying true to demographic reality means that single parents will relate to ads showing grandpa helping mother assemble her son's new bicycle. And ads often show one parent interacting with children. If the other parent is not explicitly mentioned, any parent, whether married or single, could see themselves in the ad.

Some ads deliberately target single parents. Catelli did a TV ad showing a mother having dinner with two children. Dinner is usually a family time, at least for TV families. Where was dad? Maybe he was working late, or sick in the hospital, or off fighting the Gulf War. Then again, maybe he just did not live there. The very ambivalence of the scene is what gets the attention of single parents. Of course, it would take marketing research to determine the appropriateness of such scenes for any particular product or target market. Nonetheless, there is no shortage of opportunities to play at the heart strings.

Grandparents

Demographic shifts have changed the nature of grandparenthood. Because people are living longer today, the chances of becoming a grandparent have increased. In a book entitled *The American Grandparent*, Andrew Cherlin and Frank Furstenberg, Jr. say that the chances of becoming a grandparent before death for people born in 1870 were 37 percent for men and 42 percent for women. The chances for those born in 1930 were 63 percent for men and 77 percent for women.

In a July 1990 interview in *American Demographics* magazine, Joe Fowler of the National Geographic Society said the share of grandparents buying its children's publications has increased. Likewise, over the past four years, Grandtravel, a division of The Ticket Counter travel agency in Chevy Chase, Maryland, received about 15,000 calls from grandparents for information on vacations designed for grandparents and grandchildren. The strength of the demand is even more impressive when you consider that Grandtravel spent nothing on advertising.

Most divorces create at least one "estranged" grandparent, especially since the risk of divorce is greater among younger couples, who are likely to have living parents. Grandparents divorced from their grandchildren often feel a great yearning for contact. Ads showing grandparents with grandchildren generate positive emotions anyway, but the unfulfilled needs of estranged grandparents make such themes doubly effective. The greater the physical separation among relatives, the greater the impact of advertising that portrays family togetherness.

▶ Extending Your Reach to Extended Families

The greater the physical separation among relatives, the greater the impact of advertising that portrays family togetherness.

Blended families are invisible but common. You have to know their personal history to know they are blended. The relationships among the different parts of a blended family, especially between stepsiblings, can be full of repressed anger. Products or services aimed at solving intrafamilial conflict might be especially attractive to blended families. Ads portraying such benefits can, for example, show sibling conflict and its resolution.

Children in blended families may have up to eight grandparents. Does your product sell through grandchildren? Is it the type of product that can be added to, like Lego® and Barbie™, by different gift givers? If so, blended families might be of special interest to you. Can you take a product, such as an educational savings fund, and open it to all grandparents?

Summing It Up

There will be a lag time before the new importance of the family is reflected in the household compositions of assimilated mainstream Americans. Sociologists attribute such lags to the time it takes to develop new normative scripts. The harbingers of the new focus on the family will appear in people's values first and in their living arrangements last. The period in the middle might well be the best time to adopt a family-marketing strategy. It is a time when advertising can be aspirational. Right now, family marketing can help people translate their values into new behaviors, including purchase behaviors.

Diversity does not mean the absence of common emotional ground. Good family-theme advertising deals with timeless universal tensions, hopes, anxieties, and delights of family life, and connects a product or service to functional family outcomes.

Family and household diversity is neither desirable nor undesirable in itself. All greater diversity does is alter the strategies needed to exploit marketing opportunities. At this point in American history, the satisfaction of family-related social needs is at an all-time low. The practical advertising implication is to link the product to the fulfillment of those needs. Today, staying in tune with customers on an emotional level means practicing family marketing.

REFERENCES

Balcom, Susan. "Talking Barbie Has Feminists Up in Arms." *The Vancouver Sun,* October 14, 1992, p. A3.

Blackston, Max. "Brand Personality." Presentation given at British Columbia Chapter of the American Marketing Association and the Professional Marketing Research Society, November 19, 1991.

Canadian Press. "Guys are Going for Groceries When They Wanna Have Fun." *The Vancouver Sun,* October 9, 1992, p. C2.

Canadian Press. "Media Momism Mode Miffs Working Moms." *The Vancouver Sun,* April 28, 1992, p. C2.

Goerne, Carrie. "New Mercedes Campaign Focuses on 'Relationships'," *Marketing News,* October 12, 1992, p. 2.

"Kids' Contact with Kith and Kin." *The Numbers News,* June 1992, p. 6.

Miller, Cyndee. "Michelob Ads Feature Women—and They're Not Wearing Bikinis." *Marketing News,* March 2, 1992, p. 2.

Montague, Bill. "Debate Brews Over Selling Beer With Sex." *USA Today,* November 15, 1991, p. 1B.

REFERENCES

Reed, David, and Martin S. Weinberg. "Premarital Coitus: Developing and Established Sexual Scripts." *Social Psychology Quarterly, 47,* 2, 1984, pp. 129-138.

Schlosberg, Jeremy. "Stalking the Elusive Grandparent." *American Demographics,* July 1990, p. 34.

Schlossberg, Howard. "Kid Magazine Presents Athlete in Positive Light." *Marketing News,* October 28, 1991, pp. 20-21.

Zinn, Laura, Heather Keets, and James B. Treece. "Home Alone—With $660 Billion." *Business Week,* July 29, 1991, p. 76.

About the Author

Robert Boutilier received his Ph.D. in social psychology and children's social development from the University of British Columbia in 1981. He became interested in the marketing implications of a growing North American orientation toward the family while consulting on a project to forecast social and demographic trends for the Credit Union Central of Canada in 1986. In 1987, he left his position as vice president of Criterion Research Corporation in Toronto to establish an independent marketing research practice, Boutilier and Associates, in Vancouver. Boutilier and Associates is a leader in bringing innovative approaches from social science research to marketing research practice.

Other books from
AMERICAN
DEMOGRAPHICSBOOKS.

THE BABY BUST
A Generation Comes of Age
As a generation, busters are unique in their experiences, beliefs, politics, and preferences. This is the first statistical biography of this generation. It tells their story through demographics, opinion polls, expert analysis, anecdotes, and the indispensable comments and experiences of busters themselves.

CAPTURING CUSTOMERS
How to Target the Hottest Markets of the '90s
Find out how to use consumer information to identify opportunities in nearly every market niche.

BEYOND MIND GAMES
The Marketing Power of Psychographics
The first book that details what psychographics is, where it came from, and how you can use it.

SELLING THE STORY
The Layman's Guide to Collecting and
Communicating Demographic Information
A handbook offering a crash course in demography and solid instruction in writing about numbers. Learn how to use numbers carefully, how to avoid misusing them, and how to bring cold numbers to life by relating them to real people.

THE SEASONS OF BUSINESS
The Marketer's Guide to Consumer Behavior
Learn which demographic groups are the principle players and which consumer concerns are most pressing in each marketing season.

DESKTOP MARKETING
Lessons from America's Best

Dozens of case studies show you how top corporations in all types of industries use today's technology to find tomorrow's customers.

THE INSIDER'S GUIDE TO DEMOGRAPHIC KNOW-HOW
How to Find, Analyze, and Use
Information About Your Customers

A comprehensive directory, explaining where to find the data you need, often at little or no cost. Now in its third edition.

HEALTH CARE CONSUMERS IN THE 1990S
A Handbook of Trends, Techniques, and
Information Sources for Health Care Executives

This handbook makes the connection between demographic realities and related health care issues. It will help you define your target market and carve out a niche that you can serve profitably and effectively.

Also from American Demographics

American Demographics magazine is your guide to understanding today's consumer marketplace. It does more than report on the trends; it provides unique insights on your customers and prospects. *Annual subscription $62*

The Numbers News is a monthly newsletter about the trends defining U.S. consumer markets in the 1990s and beyond. As the population becomes increasingly diverse, you need the most up-to-date information available about demographics and consumer trends. To stay ahead of your competition, you need it first. *Annual subscription $149*

Marketing Tools Catalog is an all-inclusive source of books, topical reprint packages, slides, audio cassettes, speech transcripts, software, and other products for marketing and planning professionals. Request your free copy today!

For more information about American Demographics publications, contact our Customer Service Center at 800-828-1133.

Index

A

Abelson, Robert 99
acculturation 69
affluence 35-36
African Americans **66,** 67
AIDS 30, 49, 57
Albee, Edward 69
Allen, Woody 58
Asian Americans 16, 65, **66,**
 67-72, 76, 131-2
Asians 41-42

B

baby boomers 14-15, 19-21,
 23-25, 30, 50, 56, 58, 135, 137
bachelors 7, 10
Bass, Ellen 57
Becker, Gary xi, 43
Bell, Chip 98
Blais, Eric 28
Boesky, Ivan 50
Bot, Melanie 59
Bouvier, Leon 67
Bradshaw, John 59

C

Canada 68, 131-3, 136, 140-1,
 145, 149
 divorce rates 42
 family types 7
 fertility data 19-20
 immigration 66-7
 jobs/schooling 39
 language rights 70
 suicide rates 27
 work attitudes 52, 59
Cherlin, Andrew 151

child abuse 49, 56-57
childbirth 55-6
childcare 24, 35, 49, 60-61, 136
childless couples 4, **6,** 10, 23, 140,
 148
children 6, 26-7, 37-8, 105, 133,
 136-9, 146-9
children's rights 13, 56
cocooning 135-6
Cohen, Allan 59
Corfman, Kim 101
consumer preferences 86-7
critical-incident technique 119-20
Curry, David 101, 104

D

Davis, Harry 97
Davis, Laura 57
decisionmaking
 in purchasing 4-5, 8-9, 43,
  84-5, 87, 89, 93-8, 100-103,
  114-9, 133
 model 83-5
demographics ix, 38, 88-9, 94,
 112-3, 151
divorce ix, xi, 8, 16, 26-30, 38,
 40, 42-3, 49, 56, 151-2
Doherty, William J. 11-13, 48
Draper, Thomas 126

E

Ekstrom, Karin 106
elder care 24, 30, **60,** 61
Elkind, David 12-13
employee benefits **60,** 61
empty nesters 4, 9, 125

---

bold face indicates a graph or chart

U

U.S. Bureau of the Census
5, 39-41, 112-3

V

Vetere, Arlene   115

W

Waite, Linda   14
Wallerstein, Judith   26-7
Walters, C. Glenn   125
Weinberg, Martin   57
Welniak, Edward   5
Wolfe, Tom   50
women   29-30, 50, 55
   and careers   xi, 40, 48-9, 52-3,
      55, 82, 107, 126
word-of-mouth recommendations
   141, **142**
work attitudes 52
workplace location   36-7
Wurtzel, Susan   115

Z

Zemke, Ron   98